Organisational Mindfulness

A How to Guide

Andrew McNeill

A CIP catalogue record for this book is available from the British Library

ISBN: 978-1-9162611-1-2

Cover illustrations by: Holly Lines

Dedication

This book is dedicated to anyone who has been in a
meeting and felt that it could be more inspiring.

Acknowledgements

I have to thank my wife Ruth and children, Lauren and Alex, for supporting me as I stepped away from a wonderfully sensible, normal and well-paid job to try and write about organisational mindfulness: despite the endless and (sometimes) hilarious teasing; the support, patience and kindness you have shown me, have made this possible. I must thank Vajragupta who was there when I needed him most and, having been a friend since I was 12, pointed me in the direction of mindfulness when I reached an unhappy 42. Thank you as well to Vishvapani, Paolo Quattrone and Jon Cowell, who took the time to join me for a two-day workshop in 2014, where we had one of the most inspiring conversations, I have ever been part of. It was that conversation that made me feel there was something in this idea. Paolo's work has been particularly influential, as I have said throughout the book. Finally, I would like to thank the various teams I have worked with over the years, who have tolerated me (sometimes through gritted teeth) banging on about mindfulness: without your support and challenge, this book may never have been written.

To contact the author

The ideas set out in this book are intended to help you bring mindfulness to your organisation. If you would like to contact me to discuss any of the ideas in the book, or see whether my organisation Lines of Sight, can help yours, e mail me at andrew.mcneill@linesofsight.org It would be great to hear from you and to see if we can help.

Contents

Preface

Why Organisational Mindfulness?

Have you ever felt anxious, fearful or furious at work? If
you have ever had these feelings and looked back on your
day and thought those feelings were out of control, then
this book may have a few thoughts that could help you,
your team and even your whole organisation. The basic
idea is that we have not evolved psychologically, or
physiologically, to deal with the modern world. Our work
life in particular puts us in a series of alien scenarios. Long
meetings with rivals, where we need to be polite and at
the same time get the balance of assertiveness right; one-
to-ones with a manager who knows less than you do and
even the praise from a boss you admire, which you think
is entirely unjustified, but leaves you feeling
disproportionately euphoric.

In this book I do not try to explain in detail how
mindfulness works – other authors are far better placed
to do this. I do not suggest that mindfulness is a silver
bullet to all the world's ills; I do not believe this to be
true. I do not even set out much evidence to support the
fact that mindfulness can have a positive impact on
individuals and groups: other publications have done this
analysis and with over 4,000 studies into the benefits or
otherwise of mindfulness, there is a lot of material out
there already.

What I do here is set out what I believe mindfulness can do for teams and organisations. I describe what an organisation that has adopted mindfulness at a cultural level might look like and then I set out how a person might introduce organisational mindfulness in their workplace.

This book is intended for leaders and team members of commercial enterprises, small and medium-sized businesses, public sector and third sector organisations. I intentionally use the word organisation throughout the text, to avoid drawing distinctions between different types of workplace or sector. Of course, different organisations face different challenges, but this introductory work is intended to provide some broad guidance on what organisational mindfulness is, why you might benefit from its introduction in your workplace and how you might go about implementing it.

The intention is to be practical and pragmatic. This book does not attempt to be a spiritual guide. My background is project and programme leadership and I am not qualified to talk on spiritual matters. But I do have 20 years' experience of leadership and understand the stress and pain that dysfunctional organisations can cause individuals and teams. I have also seen first-hand the transformational impact of introducing some basic, pragmatic mindfulness techniques to an organisation.

There are a surprisingly large number of chapters, but to my mind, mercifully few words in each one. It is intended for reading by people who don't really have time to read, but have maybe heard something about mindfulness and want to know more, or who know a lot about mindfulness for the individual and would like to explore how it might be applied in the workplace.

Towards the end of the book, I stray away from the workplace just a little to dip into ideas of work—life balance and how these same ideas might help in your non-work life, but I have tried as hard as possible to keep this in the office. It's just like work, mindfulness doesn't always stay there.

This book does not try and pretend that the implementation of organisational mindfulness is easy. Whilst it might be where you work, I suspect many will still face scepticism. But my experience has convinced me that this is something worth doing. The implementation of organisational mindfulness reduces stress, enhances collaboration, improves creativity and I believe increases the chances of successful delivery.

I hope you find this an interesting read. I hope you decide to explore further. If you do and you decide to implement organisational mindfulness where you work, you will be one of an increasing number of people trying to improve their workplaces in a truly radical way.

1   Why mindfulness: what is it, how did it work and what did it do?

I have worked in senior leadership for over 15 years. About seven years ago, the wheels well and truly came off. My behaviour at work and at home was erratic, my ability to concentrate was almost non-existent, I was overweight, drinking way too much and was, above all, isolated and scared. I reached out to a dear school friend of mine who happens to be a Buddhist priest (I strongly recommend everyone should have a friend who is a Buddhist priest) and he suggested that I try a mindfulness retreat. I did, and there was something about that weekend that resonated.

I decided to explore mindfulness further; I have now been practising for seven years and have trained to become a mindfulness coach. But during this journey, I have continued to work in high-pressured conventional workplaces.

At the most basic level, what do we mean by mindfulness? My favourite and often-used definition is:

"A particular way of paying attention: on purpose, in the present moment, and non-judgmentally." Jon Kabat-Zinn

Another way I have described it is to simply bring your attention to something. My friend and fellow mindfulness coach, Lucas den Engelsman, describes how we might go to the gym to become able to run a further distance, or to lift heavier weights. Similarly, mindfulness can provide a way to practise to improve our attention.

This idea of just bringing your attention to something was helpful for me when I started out with mindfulness. It demystified it. I am aware I have to pay attention at times and I have also, since I have been a child, been aware of the limitations of my attention span. What I have discovered through practising mindfulness is that first, I very often do not have my attention directed at all – it flits around all over the place and can easily alight on negative or unhelpful thoughts – and second, that I can do something about that! I can choose where to place my attention. This may seem self-evident, but it is something I had certainly lost the capacity to do a few years back and mindfulness has helped me enormously to gain or regain that ability.

So, if mindfulness is basically a way that we can improve our ability to direct our attention, then it seems logical that we can apply it to practical as well as more prosaic things. Mindful listening in conversations, mindful planning, mindful delivery: being able to bring our attention in a healthy way to what we are doing as well as finding the balance with our attention and using this skill to bring our attention away from the task in hand or unhelpful thoughts.

Initially, I bought one of the many great books on mindfulness and started to try and apply the advice in that book for myself. I found a regular time of the day that I could practise, relatively free from disturbances (for me, that meant getting up for work 20 minutes earlier) and just sat quietly bringing my attention to my breath.

Every time my mind wandered (which was, and still can be, pretty much all of the time) I gently brought my attention back to my breath. I noticed the movement in my body, from my shoulders rising and falling to the changes in my belly and back.

I began to find that movement and the sense of nourishment to be soothing, calming. My mind was still incredibly active, but I had something to bring my attention to – away from whatever thoughts were plaguing me that morning.

The repetition of this practice started to put a little distance between me and my thoughts. I started to be able to almost look at my thoughts as they developed and as they faded. They were less all-consuming and something that I started to see as being separate from me. For me, this made them less powerful. The thoughts and the franticness of my mind started to diminish a little and it felt that I had started to build a toolkit to help me deal with a problem that I had faced for most of my life, even as a child.

This started to bear fruit at work quickly too. The sort of anxiety that I was very used to at work began to affect me less and when it was really on me, I was able to remember that those thoughts were just that, thoughts. They did not have the same power that they had before. I could start to see them for what they were, even in the middle of a meeting or conversation with a difficult boss, stroppy peer or exasperating member of staff.

It felt like other people started to notice the change before I did. I will never forget when I fully realised the power of mindfulness on the way that I was behaving in the office. As per normal, I was in the middle of a particularly stressful piece of work and I was by the photocopier. A colleague came up to me and after the usual chat said, "You are always so serene." Now, apart from this not being a word that I would have associated with what was actually going on in my head, the fact that, to her, I came across as being serene was astonishing. This was a man who only one year earlier was racked with fear, self-doubt and stress. No one, absolutely no one, would have described me as being serene. It's also quite a specific word. Not calm or chilled. But serene. You may be able to tell that I'm still struck by this.

The part of the process that I found odd was that most of the time, during the day, I was not actively trying to be mindful. This profound difference in my demeanour and personal experience was being delivered for me largely by the 20-minute practice in the mornings. I have since learned that this can be advanced much further by bringing short practices into my daily life. This meant that I could actively start to manage my mind, or at least where my attention fell and the quality of the attention. This was another significant upgrade to the toolkit.

To explain, one of the things that I was learning was to be kind to myself when I was practising. There was no point in getting cross with my mind for wandering ... wandering was (and is) what my mind is built to do.

It is great at it, that is how I can manage to traverse such a complex environment mostly safely; my mind is out there checking the latest information: is this a road, is there a car, am I late, am I hungry. Lots going on. To then sit quietly and bring my attention to one thing, the breath ... that's pretty odd for my untrained mind. So, if I get cross that, when my mind wanders, I have not experienced the perfect practice, then I am really not being very fair on my mind and even more than that, my frustration will not help the practice. When I bring my wandering mind back to the breath, I have learned to do so with kindness and not to immediately jump to admonishment.

Also, as my attention was settling on my breath, I was learning that it should not be judgmental. It was important to just experience the breath for what it was at that time. So, not to be concerned that it was shallow or deep, fast or slow. Not to judge the experience, just to experience the experience.

This may seem like it would only have an impact on the quality of the meditation that I was trying to do, but it soon started to impact on the way I was dealing with stressful or joyful situations at work. If someone said something with which I did not agree, instead of immediately judging that they were wrong and then thinking about how I could beat them to get my way, I started to look at what was being said far more dispassionately.

I started to actually listen to what people were saying and then responding to what was being said, rather than reacting to a possible threat. And that kindness stuff didn't mean that I started to agree with everyone (which would be odd) but it started to mean that I started to see even the most aggressive adversaries with a scintilla of compassion. This has a very surprising effect; they became (in my mind) less powerful, less dominating. Instead of being put on the defensive by a proposition that I knew I would disagree with and resenting and either fearing or plotting against (or both) the proponent of the idea that was evidently wrong, I started to actually hear the proposition and then decide rationally whether I agreed with the proposition or not. If I disagreed with the proposition, I had a reason why and made my case, more calmly, more effectively.

The practice started to spread subtly and incrementally into the way I felt and behaved at work. I had a healthier relationship with my thoughts; I could start to see them for what they were, rather than be dominated by them. I was able to approach my decision making with less pre-judgement and start to apply my experience and professional judgement instead and I was better able to deal with the people in the team, whether adversary or supporter.

The longer I practised, the more these effects started to be noticeable to me, let alone to my co-workers. I noticed that I was coming out of stressful meetings that would have floored me before I started to practise, flustered but OK and with a sense that I had more effectively got my point across than I could have done before.

If I'd had a triumph, I was better able to retain my composure and, I guessed, my credibility with my colleagues. It was as if I was developing a regulator service for my emotions, for my mind. It wasn't numbing, it was just helping mitigate some of the extreme peaks and troughs that had been unhelpful in the way I dealt with the normal stuff that happens at work.

When I then added active practices during the day, the effect was transformative again. I could be in that difficult meeting, feel that my heart was starting to race and my breathing was becoming elevated and just by noticing, just by bringing my attention to the changes, the physical effects of the anxiety would diminish and I was better able to perform. I could think more clearly, I could speak more fluently and argue more persuasively.

This wasn't a passive step back away from the world to an easier path. This was a practical set of changes that were happening, some as a consequence of my daily formal practice, some through the application of pragmatic techniques I had picked up, and they were helping me to be more effective in the workplace and better able to look after my well-being.

On a career path evaluation, within 5½ years I had had two significant promotions and my salary had doubled. Interestingly, I was also coping with stress way beyond anything that I had experienced when the wheels originally came off. I am not claiming that that was entirely down to mindfulness. I had had 5½ years' more experience in my job. I was probably at or near peak earning age and the skills that I had developed were in demand. But I am absolutely certain that it helped!

My new ability to deal with stress more effectively and come across as calm when the pressure was on, simply made me appear more credible. The fact that I was able to look at adversaries calmly and consider their perspective with less pre-judgement, meant that I was more effective in arguing my case if I still felt my course of action was the right one. This new-found set of tools was not just helping me to survive, but was enabling me to thrive in challenging workplace situations, and employers and colleagues noticed.

Whilst the focus of this book is firmly in the workplace, the benefits to my home life and personal well-being were enormous. I was less reactive at home, resulting in fewer conflicts. My relationships with those closest to me improved which meant that I could be more helpful to them and they were more likely to listen to me. I will explore some of the whole-life benefits later in the book, but it is important to note here that the benefits from just 20 minutes' practice in the morning and some practical techniques during the course of the day were transformative outside as well as inside work.

What I then started to realise was that if mindfulness was doing this for me, it didn't just present me with some tools to improve my well-being; it also presented a set of tools that could transform my workplace. I have applied these principles and seen the results.

Behind the tools that I want to explore here is the simple thought that if we are designed to be the best survivors on the African plain, it is not surprising that we are well equipped to sense danger. If I am sitting next to you on a hilltop admiring the sunset while you are looking out for leopards, you are more likely to survive and pass on your genes than I am. I am more likely to get eaten by the leopard. But in the absence of leopards, how can I manage my physiological reaction to threat and fear in a way that helps me avoid damaging stress, helps me to keep things in proportion and even improves my performance?

I have two suggestions. First, that mindfulness can help me survive and thrive in these alien situations and second, that we can design our workplaces to support that approach. By this I don't necessarily mean having beanbags everywhere, though I am not personally against beanbags. I simply mean making mindfulness accessible, part of the culture and encouraged and supported by the way we design our processes and the products that we use.

What I aim to do in this book is introduce some techniques that I have found helpful in my work life, then explore how these might be applied in work environments and look at how we might go about implementing organisational mindfulness.

By this I mean embedding mindfulness in the way our organisations operate. My suggestion is that if we are able to do this, we can move from having a few mindful people in our organisations, who benefit from all that mindfulness can give, to having organisations that support mindfulness in the systems they apply; thereby not only do the individuals benefit from the introduction of mindfulness in the first place and the supporting infrastructure, but the organisations themselves benefit through achieving shared perspectives among their people. It's possible to overcome some competing views and increase collaboration, where there may have been silos.

This approach could transform the way we look at mindfulness, from the preserve of the individual, who knows they have an advantage and a precious toolkit, to a way to overhaul workplaces to become organisationally mindful and able to collectively enjoy the enormous and wide-ranging benefits presented by mindfulness.

It is also an approach that is practical and pragmatic but that above all has the potential to be transformational.

2   From individuals to teams

I am old enough to remember the "Lunch is for Wimps" slogan from the 1980s. There are still plenty of organisations that work with the ethos that endurance is a sign of effectiveness, that work should by its nature be hard. The rewards may be significant, so the effort should be too. There are other places that aspire to enable their people to achieve work–life balance in the belief that this is important for their people's well-being, but in reality those aspirations fall away when the work piles up and there isn't the time, money or will to deliver on that intention. There are still other places that are even more proactive in the way they help teams manage stressful situations.

We work in a range of environments, with a range of cultures, some that recognise the pressure being faced by people and some that thrive on that pressure. Regardless of the existing culture within an organisation, where either people themselves or leaders want to help manage work stress, mindfulness can be a powerful tool. I have seen mindfulness work not just for individuals working in a stressful environment, but also, by establishing a culture of collaboration and support, in a team.

I aim to look at how we might use mindfulness to help us manage the stress we face as individuals and how we might want to create mindful teams. I have also included a chapter on why I believe that many of the things we do routinely in our working lives already encourage us to be mindful. But my suggestion is that the way we use some of the processes and products that we already embrace, leads us to adopt a less mindful approach than originally intended. My ambition is that through incremental or radical change, we can get the most out of our current systems and design new ones that help support improved decision making and effectiveness.

The reality is that almost anywhere that you work, there will be times when things get tough and in fact some pressure is not necessarily a bad thing. This book is explicitly not advocating just taking it easy. Nor is it suggesting that every office, factory and shop should be fitted out with meditation benches and ambient whale song. That may be your choice and that's great, but my intention here is to be practical and pragmatic. What changes will help people improve their well-being and helps employers to reduce rates of absenteeism, increase focus on delivery, improve creativity and staff engagement.

A lot of what I propose is about balance. It is not new. Mindfulness has is routes in a 2,500-year-old tradition and most of us know that taking some time out away from a problem can sometimes help us resolve it. Expressions like "sleep on it" and "can't see the wood for the trees," reflect the fact that stepping back has been a necessary part of the human condition for so long, that it is represented in parts of our vernacular.

To go back to my experience of mindfulness: as I explained, it started with a pretty personal crisis. I needed to find tools that could help the anxiety and pressure that I was feeling on a daily basis. There was something that resonated for me in the mindfulness practices, they were surprisingly practical and although I now recognise the impact to be cumulative, at the time there seemed, for me, to be a fairly rapid short-term improvement in my stress levels too. About one year into my practice, I had the opportunity to go on a residential course for senior programme managers. The Major Project Leaders Academy (MPLA) is an outstanding and challenging course that takes about 18 months to complete and requires three-week-long residential stays. The course is run by Oxford University and covers a very wide range of topics including leadership. Initially, I decided to keep my 'hippy' inclinations to myself and not mention how I use mindfulness. But three-week-long periods sharing long days in the lecture hall and evenings in the bar, tended to break down my barriers. In a couple of conversations, the issue of stress came up and the sheer pressure of being a senior leader. I mentioned mindfulness, fully expecting people to smile politely (or not) and to move on. But many of the people on the course wanted to know more. They spotted the possibility that this could be a helpful tool. We were given the option at the end of the second week to use some of the final week to explore a topic of our choice in some more depth. The delegates asked if I could arrange a session on mindfulness. At the time, I felt wholly unqualified to lead such a course myself, so I reached out to my dear Buddhist school friend, who said no. Which I thought was singularly un-Buddhist of him. But he did offer me the name of a friend of his, Vishvapani, who very kindly agreed and came along and did an hour-long session for us, introducing some of the ideas behind mindfulness and giving us a shared led practice session. Of the 30 senior project leaders in the room, 29 said that they had got something positive from the experience and the thirtieth was polite.

This whole process convinced me that there was an appetite and that mindfulness resonated with a fair proportion of a senior leadership audience.

Much encouraged, I returned to my workplace and with a fellow mindfulness practitioner, Nicola Lowit, established a weekly mindfulness drop-in session. To be completely honest, I doubt that I would have had the courage to have started this without Nicola and I'm pretty sure it was her idea. At this point, I was a senior leader attending executive board meetings on a monthly basis and leading a substantial team. But the prospect of leading a group of co-workers in some mindfulness practice was totally outside my comfort zone. It felt like a complete clash of cultures, in a stark office and with people whom I faced at work, rather than personal challenges. But as we're going to explore later in the book, I am coming to the conclusion that my experience is my experience, whether that is in work or at home, so that distinction is fairly artificial and so too was the barrier in my mind between mindfulness being about personal well-being and about how work teams behave and deliver effectively. The other lesson from this was that having overcome the fear, the response was astonishing, extremely positive and encouraging. The group itself was sustained by Nicola for years after I left the organisation. This experience also made me start to think about how we might broaden access to the techniques offered by mindfulness practice for individuals and for teams.

From then on, wherever I have worked I have introduced mindfulness to the team and tried to embed it into the practices of the workplace. Where we have managed to introduce and embed mindfulness into the DNA of the programme, it has helped individuals to manage their stress more effectively, established a more collaborative approach among the senior leadership team and led to greater levels of creativity in our decision making.

These experiences have convinced me that mindfulness can be used not just by individuals to manage their own stress and improve their own well-being, but that it can be placed at the heart of the design of any team, made part of its culture and transform the way the team works.

3   Programme management – and other mindful practices

As my core trade/profession is project and programme management, it involves a set of products (documents) and processes with which I am very familiar. Highlight reports, risk registers, programme board meetings have been my business for about 25 years. It was from my understanding of project management that my recognition that mindfulness could be embedded into a workplace at a structural level emerged. I would stress at this point that to my mind almost any activity can be discussed in terms of a project. From making a cup of team, to the UK's HS2. There are specific definitions, about temporary organisations and so on, but to me all a project is, is a way of organising activity.

You want to achieve something. You work out what it is. The way you want to achieve it. What resources will you need, when? What will be delivered, when? You plan out what activity needs to happen in which order. You consider in advance what might go wrong and how can you avoid those things from happening. You set up some way of gathering information, so you know if you are on track, or if you need to do something a bit differently. You have a structure for decision making, so as things go along, you can check whether your thinking is right. And once it's done, you check whether the project did what it was supposed to and gather some more information about how it went.

That's it. Don't tell anyone, but it is not complicated. It's just really hard to do it, when lots of senior people want

you to deliver the impossible, yesterday, with no money
...

But in essence it is just: vision, cost-benefit analysis, plan (including resources), risk and issue management, reporting, evaluation and lessons learnt.

Best example I can think of is a holiday. You decide whether you want sun or snow, excitement or relaxation, how long for and when in the year. There you go, you have a vision. If you're on your own, you just decide this is something you want to do; if you have a partner, you may decide together that this is something you are going to do. That's your mandate. You then work out how you might achieve it, checking out websites and maybe going to a travel agent. That's the discovery phase. Then, having worked out how you want to go about achieving your vision (maybe two weeks in Lanzarote) you plan it: when can you get time off work, when can you go to the travel agents, have you got enough money to pay for it now, or do you want to pay in instalments – initiation. Then you go along and buy the holiday and now you are already into implementation, because you have to make sure you make any instalments, you are getting your passports organised, eventually packing and you are on your flight. Having implemented the delivery of your project (holiday) you return and look through the pictures and talk about it (possibly endlessly to your friends). Lessons learned. From your lessons learned you decide that next year you want to go to Iceland for a city break ...

We all run pretty major projects all the time, so why then is there an entire industry around project management with almost as many books written about the subject as mindfulness?

If I was super-cynical I would say, so that people like me could earn a living by mystifying something that is very straightforward. But actually applying these principles is really challenging, especially when they need to be sustained over long periods of time with tactical challenges emerging on a daily basis. To misquote Christina Feldman: "Project management is neither difficult nor complex; remembering to project manage is the great challenge."

This is perhaps the first uncanny parallel between project management and mindfulness.

But the most startling parallel for me was the realisation that if mindfulness is simply the exercise of choice in where we place our attention, then it is precisely what project managers, project management offices and project boards do on a daily basis.

The enormous advantage of project management over delivering an activity without project management structures and disciplines, is that project management (if done well) requires the leaders of the delivery activity and those responsible for the money funding that activity, to pay attention to what is going on. This happens in a number of different ways, the risk reporting perhaps being the most dramatic, and the project board being the most strategic.

A risk is just anything that could impact on the delivery of a project. Risk assessment demands that the risk or project manager identify what those things may be and then dispassionately assess the likelihood of those things happening. Having agreed with the board the list of risks, the assessment of their likelihood and what can be done to make them less likely to happen (mitigation), a tolerance must be agreed, in other words, how much more likely can the thing get, before it is escalated and reported up the line. To use the holiday example, the risk is that you need to apply for a new passport and this doesn't arrive in time. The mitigation is to pay for an expedited application. The milestone is that the passport is expected one month ahead of the date of the flight. The tolerance is that the passport can arrive one week later than expected, the escalation is to tell your partner that it is late and you both have to start phoning the passport office.

The point here is that the project manager, or you, have to make a dispassionate (non-judgmental) assessment of the risk and what can be done to avoid it. It is no good saying "it'll be fine" or "there's no point in trying to go on holiday" if you haven't got a passport six months in advance of the leaving date. Neither are necessarily true. You need to bring your attention to the matter at hand and achieve as accurate an assessment of the risks as you can.

Another example is the project board. This is the set-piece moment when (at regular intervals) the people responsible for the delivery of the project report to the people ultimately accountable for the delivery of the project, including spending the money and realising the benefits. This is even more intriguing, in that it is an exercise in shared collective attention or mindfulness.

We can go one stage further and look at some of the qualities required for this shared attention to be effective: it needs to be dispassionate and focussed on the current situation, not the troubles of the past or the consequences of failure or success. The question in essence for the board at each meeting is, does this project still stack up? Is it on track to deliver? Do we need to take action to get this activity back on track?

Very often, projects that are in fact failing are allowed to continue, despite mounting costs or delay, because people are thinking about what may or may not happen if the project is stopped. The damage to a senior person's reputation, the personal belief and emotional investment in a project, the sense that the project is an intrinsically good thing to do. This can result in the project not being stopped, or changed and even more money being committed, which as a consequence makes it even harder to close down the project.

If we consider our other definition of mindfulness – "non-judgmental present moment awareness" – I cannot think of a better definition for the role of an effective project board.

The other idea that I found interesting about this comparison was that it was a shared awareness. If the board is not complete (not quorate) it is not normally empowered to make decisions. The board must have a sufficient number of key members present to consider the issues faced by the project, to be able to make decisions. This requirement, which is standard practice in a project board's terms of reference, forces the people accountable for the project's spend and delivery to have a shared awareness of progress and challenges faced by those delivering the project. One person cannot make that judgement on their own.

If it is considered routinely essential for project boards of all scales, including those of major infrastructure projects, to have moments of shared awareness of the current situation with a project, and if the most effective type of decision making is that based on evidence, rather than preconceived views, then has project management methodology not created for the twenty-first century, a mechanism that reflects the tools presented by 2,500-year-old traditions of mindfulness? What's more, can we not find examples of this type of practice in other fields, such as stock audits for wholesalers, hygiene inspections for restaurants or education authority inspections of schools?

There are numerous examples of day-to-day business life in countless sectors that require a relatively brief period of shared, non-judgmental awareness.

Returning to our holiday analogy, if we work on the scenario that there are two people involved in the decision making, are there not numerous occasions when non-judgmental present moment awareness would help? To set the vision, you may need to pause and bring your attention to what you both can agree would be a good idea. If you don't both want a beach holiday, is there a location that offers a beach and a bit of history for one of you to visit, or nice restaurants? If you don't pause to achieve a shared vision, one of you is going to feel that this holiday is not for them. On the cost and the planning (initiation), a non-judgmental or dispassionate view is well advised, unless you are happy to spend the next two years paying for it. And as for the lessons learned, again, you have to hear the view of the other person, or mistakes will be repeated.

Whether we are talking about a highly structured major project, or a summer break, the need to choose to bring our shared attention to something at key points is essential for success.

So, why does this matter, and is this not patently obvious? Well, it does sound self-evident once it is pointed out, but I would not until very recently have described these occurrences as a type of organisational mindfulness. And I would have said that, generally, mindfulness as a practice was fairly alien to most workplaces. I still think this is a fair description, not least because of the misconceptions about what mindfulness actually is. But maybe some of those misconceptions can be overcome if we accept that, in fact, shared, non-judgmental present awareness or bringing groups of people with different skills and authority together to exercise their judgment without prejudice is already something that organisations and people do all the time.

Next question: if we do this all the time, why have you written a book about bringing mindfulness into organisations? Well, my suggestion is that whilst we have logically established structures that bring our attention to things all the time, we don't always do this very well. We do it through set pieces, that can be as much about theatre and, in the worst cases (accidentally or on purpose), create distraction, rather than focus attention. The proposition is that we just might be able to improve the effectiveness of some of those processes if we enhance them with tools to bring our attention fully to the task at hand and if we expand the application of shared non-judgmental present moment awareness from the monthly board meeting to much wider areas of our working lives.

In fact, I would say that in some cases the set pieces that are designed to bring our attention to something, can on occasion have the opposite effect. They can create an illusion that attention is being brought to an issue or to a project's delivery but in fact this is just not the case. An extreme example might be when the board members are all on their mobile phones, actually in another meeting or conversation, outside the room. But this is just an extreme example. A personal lack of attention can be much more subtle than that and an institutional lack of attention can be missed by numerous individuals and can be enormously costly to the organisation.

Going back to project management, it was Paolo Quattrone who first brought my awareness to this idea. With his kind permission, I am terribly paraphrasing his thesis (which I would encourage you to explore).

At the MPLA, Paolo explained that bookkeeping had been developed by Jesuits to create a space for thought and reflection. But what we currently used it for, was simply getting to a number. The bottom line. This negated the capacity of double book accounting as a way of bringing the people of power together to make decisions about where the money was spent, in the original case Jesuit priests; in our situations, corporate or project board members, head teachers and their deputies, and so on. Paolo went on to say that we did the same thing in our project management. At this point in his presentation, I started to feel quite unwell ... I realised that I had spent a large part of my career as a project, programme manager producing reports for boards. These reports had never intentionally disguised the facts. I prided myself on my probity. But these reports were also highly professional, even fairly slick. This gave the impression to very busy board members that matters were well in hand. That more junior people had a grip. Whilst this was undoubtedly true, what these products might have failed to do was support an atmosphere of shared attention (or non-judgmental present moment awareness).

Just a question, but does this sound familiar to your experience? Your board never has enough time to consider the entire agenda; there are often board members on their phones, texting or reading messages; there are vested interests or emotional investments being voiced? Do the reports presented to the board and the accompanying presentations reinforce the status quo, supporting the perception that the whole organisation is very busy, and that, by and large, things are on track and good people are on it?

An alternative could be to ban mobile phones from a board meeting. To start the meeting with a three-minute practice, to have materials that creatively bring the board members' attention to the key issues at hand and to have the presentation delivered by the people who are closest to action.

Cranfield University conducted a longitudinal qualitative research study drawing on 21 in-depth interviews conducted over six months with eight leaders who had participated in Cranfield's three-day Mindful Leadership Programme. Participants were between 35–56 years old, leading teams of 3 to 1,200 employees in private and public sector organisations across Europe and the Middle East, so a real range of leaders.

There were at least three distinctive ways that mindfulness seemed to have an impact and these were some of the comments received from the participants:

Informal mindfulness practice becomes more important over time:
"My questions are different and the way I listen to the answers has changed. I now really want to hear what people say."

They are more willing to stay put in the face of difficulty:
"I breathe and think about how to move forward constructively rather than brooding on what I should have done."

They proactively promote emergent, bottom-up decisions:
"Now I make sure the real experts have a voice on decisions."

So, my suggestion is fourfold. First, we have already created structures and processes in our organisations that aspire to engender shared attention. Second, these may not always work as well as we would like. Third, the ability of individuals to bring their attention individually and collectively to the matter in hand may improve the effectiveness of these processes and finally, that these processes and those individuals could be supported by organisational mindfulness: some simple tools to help people achieve a shared moment of non-judgmental present moment awareness.

Maybe if we view the challenge of bringing mindfulness into the heart of the workplace as being one of adapting, enhancing the existing structures that we have, it all becomes a lot easier. If we recognise that what project management and other standard work practices aspire to do is very much in line with what mindfulness can achieve, then we are looking at just reaching for a low-tech pragmatic enhancement to the existing workplace environment, rather than getting the whole team to wear kaftans ...

We would not, for example, dream of rejecting as avant-garde the use of flip charts or whiteboards as tools to help us to achieve a shared awareness of the problems being identified by a team meeting. Why then would we reject the idea of starting a meeting with a three-minute breathing practice to achieve the same aim?

Similarly, anyone who has worked in an agile project environment is familiar with stand-ups where teams share the actions for the day and progress on their element of the work. (For those not familiar with the term, agile methodology is largely used in IT projects to allow for iterative development.) These daily meetings are brief and should be animated and although they can seem to be contrived when they start to be implemented, they soon become standard practice and agile project management is widely applied. They are similar in a way to daily briefings that a crisis management team would set up or that a police shift would expect as standard at the start of an evening. If, in the right setting, daily briefings are seen as being essential to effective delivery, why wouldn't daily practice be seen in the same light, particularly when the evidence shows that it can make a difference to performance?

In your organisation, for example, could you start your daily briefings with a three-minute practice?

Shared attention

There is one other point I would like to draw out of the project management and mindfulness comparison. It is the idea of shared attention: that the existing structures established by good project management are designed to force or facilitate shared attention or experience. A board meeting is not a solitary experience (unless everyone in the room is blaming you for a failure, or you have the wrong day – in which case it can feel like a very solitary experience). A board meeting should be the shared experience of those accountable and responsible for spend and delivery.

My experience of mindfulness, unless I am on a training course, is that it is a largely solitary experience. This is not unpleasant or sad. Giving myself permission to have a bit of "me time" has been essential to improving my well-being. It is, however, a fact that my personal practice normally consists of me on my own meditating for 20 minutes in the morning and then maybe stealing a few minutes' practice during the course of a working day, at my desk or walking round a park at lunch or on the way to work. I am not part of a Buddhist community and I do not currently have time to join a shared practice group. I think the excellent array of apps available to help with led meditations, perpetuate this solitary approach to practice. But what I find interesting about the example presented by project management, is that mindfulness, or present moment awareness, does not have to be solitary.

If we are serious about developing structural ways to support mindful practice in the workplace, we will be helping people to develop both a personal practice and a shared one.

So, this is the core reason for writing this book. There are many routes for people to find and develop a personal mindfulness practice. The development of those routes is (in my view) to be applauded. The increase in accessibility to mindfulness frankly just makes personal practice less weird. There are thousands of studies that prove that mindfulness helps people with their own well-being and performance and therefore is likely to enhance the ability of an organisation to deliver its objectives, whether that is excellent blue-light services or a profit.

But if we look objectively at many of our business practices, they are already designed to achieve a shared pause and shared attention. This approach is already key to success; that's why large companies spend lots of money on them. So, if this is already part of our corporate and organisational culture and if more and more of our people are taking up mindfulness as a way to enhance their ability to perform, why can't we bring the two together? Why can't we simply enhance our existing culture and processes with some small tweaks and changes that could lead to organisational mindfulness. The aim being to support those who want to develop their personal practice, but more than that even! To build on and enhance the shared attention that organisations *already* strive for on a daily basis.

4   Potential benefits of organisational mindfulness

In the 1990s I was working at a medium-sized law firm. It was a great opportunity, but I couldn't see it. I was frustrated with my job, with myself, with my life (I was 22). I called a friend and plaintively asked, "Jim, do you think people are naturally apathetic?" Jim laughed. I was a bit miffed and asked him what he was laughing at. "I'm surprised you could be bothered to pick up the phone and ask the question" he said.

If you are interested in mindfulness and thinking about trying to introduce it to your workplace, the truth is it would almost certainly be easier to keep that to yourself, to develop your own personal practice and reap your own benefits. Certainly, in the UK, although it is rapidly getting more widely accepted, it is still seen as being a bit odd. The offices in which I have worked are normally high-pressured environments with people just trying to get the job done as effectively as they possibly can. They can also often be quite cynical places with people keen to blame each other for mistakes or problems, rather than actually address the problems.

You may think that bringing in something that might be seen as being really novel could mark you out for ridicule or unwelcome attention. People may also not thank you for bringing them something else to consider while they already have a stack of things with which to deal. If you are the boss, you may worry that it may impact on your credibility and undermine your authority.

Well, all of these things are possible. But they haven't happened yet.

If we look at the evidence, there are over 4,000 studies that demonstrate that mindfulness can help to reduce sick absence, improve well-being, enhance creativity and cognitive ability and improve relationships between staff members. You may also want to look at "Building the Case for Mindfulness" by the UK Mindfulness Initiative, which is great source of information about why mindfulness may be worth thinking about.

The bottom line is that the beneficial impacts of mindfulness have been known for a very long time. Scientific rigour has been brought to bear and found that the benefits are real and measurable. So, the application or use of mindfulness is no longer the preserve of the hippies, the Buddhists and the survivors of the sixties. The choice to find out more and to practise mindfulness is logical in the same way that taking regular moderate exercise is logical. There is research that tells us that this activity is good for us. Equally, just like taking regular moderate exercise, it is not easy for most of us to get into the habit. It is easier to just buy bigger clothes.

To bring mindfulness to your workplace you will be faced with the challenge of your own concerns about how it might be perceived and the consequences for you of doing this, as well as the possible inertia of your colleagues once you get underway; we will explore the challenges of implementing mindfulness in your workplace later. For now, it is fair to accept that it is perfectly reasonable to be put off by the sense of risk, whether real or imagined, and the scale of the challenge.

But there is an amazing prize on offer.

Many of us may be familiar with the issue of stress in the workplace and the impact on our organisations and it is absolutely right that we should celebrate that mindfulness can help reduce stress. The World Health Organisation has described stress as the health epidemic of the 21st century, with the UK's Health and Safety Executive stating in 2017 that half a million people in the UK reported that work-related stress was making them ill, which means that nearly 57% of UK sick days are caused by stress.

But it does not stop there. Mindfulness can help people improve their cognitive ability and operate more effectively and collaboratively in teams. As already mentioned, the tools offered by mindfulness need not be reserved for those who are struggling or recovering. Mindfulness can also help people stay well and avoid the negative impacts of stress and can simply help people maximise their potential. All of this can benefit individuals of course, but it can also benefit organisations.

We are going to explore the use of a business case, but the overheads of a mindfulness programme are relatively low. You don't have to buy and pay to have equipment installed (no gym required) or to remodel your office. It is cheap, pragmatic and doesn't even take up much time! But the benefits in reduced sick absence, improved performance and better collaboration, could be substantial.

It is also timely. Many schools now have mindfulness programmes. This was unheard of in the 1970s and 80s. If the next generation are used to mindfulness and are looking to work in progressive working environments, what will the top employers need to be offering? I would suggest that as well as great remuneration packages, good holiday allowances and possibly healthcare, the next generation will be looking for employers who take well-being seriously and mindfulness can be a significant part of that offer. If you are prepared to explore the introduction of mindfulness now, you may draw nearer to the industry leaders and quite rapidly get your organisation in a better position to be ready for the graduates of the future.

But it is not just millennials who will expect well-being programmes or who see mindfulness as being mainstream rather than alternative. In the UK in February 2019, despite the height of the parliamentary merriment that was Brexit, a question was asked in Prime Minister's Questions about mindfulness. For the mother of parliaments to have a question raised about mindfulness, felt like a benchmark of acceptability.

Indeed, the UK Parliament has a well-established all-party parliamentary group (APPG) on mindfulness. But before we get distracted by the UK Parliament and all its history, consider that Google have had a mindfulness programme for years as have Jaguar Land Rover, the Leeds Building Society, GlaxoSmithKline, and so on and so on. Mindfulness is no longer novel. It is widely accepted. And if it is being seen as best practice in these businesses, should you not consider it for yours?

If you want to see the benefits of mindfulness affect your workplace, see the teams you lead or are part of become happier, more resilient, take less time off for sick leave, become more creative and improve their ability to maintain their attention, then it might be worth considering how you could bring mindfulness into your workplace.

So, if it:

1) can save you money (e.g. by reducing sick leave)
2) improves your people's ability to perform
3) improves your attractiveness to the most promising recruits
4) is cheap to implement
5) is being done by your competitors

does the question change from "why bother", to "can I afford not to"?

5 What might a mindful organisation look like?

Before launching into how we implement this change, it might be worth looking at a vision of what your organisation might look like if it were to become mindful. As I've said, for me this had to be pragmatic and it had to improve delivery. I devised the model below to try and show board-level leaders how a mindful organisation might be different in practice.

Mindful about why we are doing this	Mindful about each other
Mindful about delivery	Mindful about ourselves

The four quadrants are important because they demonstrate balance. Employers and bosses have every justifiable reason to expect delivery, most of us want to deliver. Evidence suggests that delivery can be supported by mindfulness, but there may well be a misconception that mindfulness is purely about well-being or purely about bringing our attention to the ethereal and that mindfulness is all a bit esoteric.

Enabling people to improve their well-being improves delivery. But being clear that mindfulness is about delivery on its own merits as well as well-being, is important. If we are inclined to try and introduce mindfulness to our workplace, it helps makes it clear that we are after balance and that this approach can be applied to help well people deliver more effectively, as well as support those of us who are struggling.

In addition to showing that we are after balance and to demonstrate the practical nature of mindfulness, the model draws attention to the significant benefits mindfulness can have for well people. This set of tools need not be the exclusive preserve of those who are recovering from burnout. The gym can help you stay fit and keep you getting into your slim-fit jeans, it is not just there to help you lose the weight and get back into them. It is up to us how we use these tools and they can be made available to all.

Mindful about why we are doing this

It is easy to lose track of why we started to do something. This is true in our personal lives as well as in our professional lives. In large projects and programmes, the immediate pressure to hit a particular deadline or prepare for a board meeting can routinely blot out the reason that the project or programme was established. Most activities, whether they are a specific project or programme or another type of organisation, have a clear reason to exist. There is a defined aim. It could be to make money, to save money, to deliver services or build a structure. Whatever the activity, most will start with a purpose. If we lose track of why we are doing something, the impact can be catastrophic. We can start to invest our energies in ways that do not help achieve the goal, we can lose sight of the overall target delivery date, while focussing on an immediate one, we can even end up delivering the wrong thing.

That's why it was important for me, as a programme leader, to include being mindful of why we are doing this activity as part of the model. We have to take a step back from time to time to reflect on what was the original mission, are we doing the right things to achieve that mission and is it still the right mission. If we do this, we are able to decide whether the mission is still relevant or whether we should be doing something different. We should be able to apply our resources to the most effective actions and determine whether we are on track and take action to get back on track, if we are not.

Part of this links to the value of thinking of programme management as a mindful activity and I will explore this further later, but there is also something here about being able to be dispassionate, and to detach emotionally from some activities. Leaders of projects and programmes or organisations and those working in any activity can get enormously attached to an activity. Having invested skills and time on a course of action, it is entirely natural to not want it to be stopped or told that what you are doing is wrong or needs to be adjusted. This sense of emotional attachment, coupled with the personal threat implicit in our current occupation being brought to an end or significantly changed, can cause any of us to start to defend activities that are not actually productive or effective. Bringing our attention to the vision behind the activity and away from our emotional attachment to the current activity, is a powerful way to help us make dispassionate decisions based on evidence and empower us to change direction or even stop an activity and start doing something new.

Mindful about delivery

This is another point about balance and the practical nature of mindfulness. When any of us are asked to complete tasks, we may struggle to stay focussed. If we are excited by the task and absolutely believe in it, then it may be easier, but even then the prospect of getting home and back to the box set or some other more potent personal distraction, can take our attention away. If the task is tedious, or if we are doing it without conviction, focus can be even more illusive.

Mindfulness can simply help ourselves and our teams to more effectively choose where our attention is placed. Regular mindfulness practice, like regular attendance at the gym, can just improve our ability to focus and this can help us to be more effective.

Moving from the individual to the team perspective, one of the most challenging things for a programme manager is to keep people focussed on the plan. New instructions can arrive from senior sources, or team members get distracted by other requests. Once an activity and a plan has been agreed, success depends on taking the actions necessary to deliver the plan. Bringing our attention to what has to happen next and doing that work.

This does not contradict the earlier point about being willing to change direction. Plans are there to change, but that choice to flex or change the plan needs to be a conscious one. It requires dispassionate attention and on a day-to-day basis teams need to be clear on what needs to be done next and if that has changed, what the new tasks are. If not, the end goal will not be delivered. It is worth considering that the more pressured the environment, the quicker priorities or activities might change and the more important dispassionate, conscious decision making becomes.

Mindful about each other

In the most intense environments, it is very easy to lose sight of the people who are right next to you. If people are struggling with exhaustion or stress they may not even see it themselves. Team members may think they are being super-diligent, or may fear the consequences of admitting they are at the end of their tether. The best teams that I have worked in, are the ones where people, regardless of seniority, feel able to say: "are you OK?".

The power of looking out for each other can be enormous. Not only can it build the sense of belonging and engagement in the team, it can avoid burnout for team members with the resultant loss in productivity as replacements or interim solutions are sought.

But, to be able to effectively look out for our colleagues we have to bring our attention to their well-being. This can be genuinely hard as we are often wrapped up in our own work and personal lives and find it hard enough to consider how we ourselves are doing.

We may also have to bring our attention to the well-being of someone with whom we don't particularly get along. But going back to my preferred definition for mindfulness – *non-judgmental, present moment awareness* – if we are, in that moment, aware that someone is struggling and we can park our own judgement about that person, we may be able to either engage with them or get someone else to do so and help them avoid burning out or needing time away. This in turn helps us as a team member.

Mindful about ourselves

The oxygen mask analogy will be familiar to many of you, but I've found it an incredibly graphic and powerful way to remind myself that if I am going to help other people, I have to look after myself first. For anyone not familiar, it is simply the advice that you may have received on any plane before take-off. In the unlikely event that the oxygen masks come down, please put the mask on yourself, before you attempt to help anyone else, including your child. For a long time, this was anathema to me. Both as a member of a team, and even more so as a leader, I felt obligated to stay until the end, to look after those in my command, and felt negligent if I stepped away. The idea of putting others before ourselves can be deeply ingrained and in and of itself it is a great sentiment, but it is only possible if we have the energy and capacity to give to other people. If we are burned-out or exhausted, we will be of no help to our colleagues or the organisation as a whole let alone those people in our personal life. In essence, looking after yourself can be a selfless act if it means that you are ready and able to support those around you.

This doesn't mean that there aren't plenty of times when practically, pragmatically, we have to "dig deep" and stay late, or go to that meeting that we were dreading, but if we do these things with a plan to make that sustainable, then we may be present in the team for longer and able to do those extra tough things without needing periods of time away to recharge.

6   If you tried this, what might success look like?

If we have some understanding of what mindfulness is or could be for our organisation, what are we aiming for? As I've said to pretty much every boss I've had when they hire me "what does success look like?". The value for me of asking that question is that I make sure I know what the boss wants and I can start to plan how to achieve it. It also pins the boss down, so they can't change the goalposts. It's the same here. What do we want to achieve? Once we've got a clear idea of our goals, we can test that with others, see whether they concur and eventually agree what the organisation expects.

You could aim for a complete refit of your office, with everyone sitting on cushions and really low desks … but I'm not sure that would be terribly practical or necessary or that it would comply with the local health and safety legislation. My suggestion would be to start small, but be ambitious. But you know your organisation. You may decide that going big and being radical is the best way to go.

Having had the chance to try and implement organisational mindfulness, I have some practical ideas that, if they can be achieved, would be good signs of success. This is partly to reassure you that I am not talking about extreme measures. Everything that I am suggesting I think is achievable in most organisations if there is the will.

In my most recent programme we did three key things that I believe made a difference.

Normalising

First, we started to normalise mindfulness. Nothing more challenging than that we talked about it! Just by making mention of mindfulness more frequent, it became less weird and more acceptable. Second, we found ways to share the experience of mindfulness, rather than just having lots of separate practitioners and finally, we brought it into the routine of the work.

This achieved a number of things. First, it gave permission for people who had a personal practice to share their experience and for those who were interested in mindfulness to express that interest in what had become a safe environment. Second, it moved some of our mindful practice from being separate and individual, to being a shared experience. These shared experiences were brief, but it meant that despite sometimes having competing priorities, the team that took part had a few moments of stillness that they shared together.

To be honest, I have sometimes wondered whether it was just the fact that we had shared something a bit odd and sometimes a little awkward that have made the difference. Would that have been enough to bring us closer together as a team? But I suspect this was just a small part of the story. I don't think people would have continued to take part. The final important thing we achieved was to make sure it actually happened. By integrating mindfulness into our routine, it meant that it was something we were not just talking about, but something we were practising.

All we did to achieve this normalisation initially was to talk to the team. We had an event that was designed to effectively launch the programme. The event had a number of key senior speakers in the morning. We started the afternoon with a session led by the wonderful Vishvapani, a Triratna Buddhist, teacher and broadcaster. We did a joint presentation, where I explained what mindfulness meant to me and why I thought it could be valuable to us as a group and he then introduced his perspective and led the room, of approximately 70 people, in a practice. During the course of the afternoon we ran a series of practical exercises, but kept inviting the group to complete their tasks in a mindful way. The impact was fascinating. I have been to more team events that I care to remember, but at this one there was a quieter volume, despite the numbers, and a very high ceiling! We immediately got great feedback from the participants. There were, of course, some people who did not buy into it, but many did and we had started the conversation.

The top table

The next key thing we did was to bring mindfulness into the senior team meetings. These were weekly events and at the start of each meeting, just for three minutes, those who wanted to take part had a led mindful practice. I have included here a few testimonials from fellow directors on the programme to demonstrate the sort of impact that mindfulness can have for people in high pressured environments.

I would be lying if I said that the practices always went smoothly. Occasionally, people stumbled in late to the meeting, disrupting the practice and it was all very embarrassing. But we got used to the routine and it started having a profound impact. Put at its most basic, people were present in the room. They were not still thinking about the email they were halfway through drafting, or the next meeting. More fundamentally, we had taken a few moments to bring our attention to the business of the meeting and had a shared experience as we did that, meaning that the meetings tended to be far more collaborative that other boards I have witnessed.

"Andrew introduced the concept of a mindful programme early on. It was fundamental, in an extremely busy and stressful environment, to helping us individually and collectively to stop, think, engage in key discussions and ensure our resilience. Simple practices such as five minutes of mindfulness at the start of meetings really helped us to transition from the pressure of competing demands as we came into the room, to being able to focus and collectively solve key issues as leaders. Personally, I credit mindfulness with helping to increase my resilience at a time of considerable pressure and stress."

My experience of senior teams, is that there is not always a blossoming of harmony and shared agendas. The reality is that senior leadership is hard. People are often under enormous pressure and although they work for the same organisation, they regularly have competing agendas. This, coupled with the fact that on occasion senior leaders can have egos the size of Belgium, can lead to conflict.

My experience of this team, was that it was uniquely collaborative and the testimonials support the idea that despite this being the most highly pressured environment that many of us had ever experienced, the top team worked together, looked out for each other and came through in better shape as a result. Mindfulness had made us more effective as a team and had created a shared experience, rather than a series of solitary ones. This, I am convinced, improved our decision making and at least reduced the amount of stress that we might have caused ourselves and each other.

The fact that the senior team did this, also set out a powerful message to the rest of the team. The message was about how seriously we took the task at hand and our well-being. Feedback from others across the team, was that this meant a great deal. We were not just paying lip service to the importance of well-being. We were taking active steps to look after our own well-being and therefore, it was OK for the rest of the team to do the same thing.

But again, as well as our well-being, it was important that we were doing this to improve our ability to get the job done. To improve our performance, both individually and collectively.

And it made sure that mindfulness happened! It wasn't just an aspiration, it was real and something we did together routinely at least once a week. But it is really important to note here that this was not a big ask. We were not taking large chucks of the scheduled time for the meeting on mindfulness. The cost impact was minimal, but the effect was considerable. It was also practical, no equipment required, just the guidance of someone who had sufficient experience and the expertise to introduce mindfulness. So, there is something here for me about pragmatic delivery. We are going to explore the real potential for transforming your organisation and I think this where you can maximise the benefits, but you can start small and demonstrate the value to a small group of influencers quickly with a minimal amount of investment. Being able to have such a significant impact quickly at such low cost, can help you to make your case for incremental or radical implementation of these principles.

It may not be possible to get the top team to start practising themselves, but if there is a way you can demonstrate their buy-in and that they are supporting and giving permission for people to explore mindfulness, then you will be providing the support you need for organisational mindfulness.

Deeper exploration of mindfulness

Another thing we did was to offer a more "in-depth" mindfulness training course to the team. This eight-week course was fully subscribed within hours of being advertised. I recognised that, whilst we were making great steps with our public discussion of mindfulness and senior team involvement, the level of understanding and knowledge of mindfulness was inevitably at a very surface level. My thought was that there may well be some people who wanted to explore mindfulness a bit further and this proved to be the case. The course ran in the evenings, so again the course was fully subscribed despite the requirement for people to attend in their own time.

I strongly suspect that we could have run several iterations of the course and would have been able to run many more, if it could have been accommodated in work time. The course I ran was free, but again, if the cost of the training could be met by the organisation, this would undoubtedly improve levels of participation.

Running this type of course does carry some cost, for example time out of the office for those being trained and for professional trainers to deliver the training. The market for training is maturing rapidly and increasingly you can find effective training that can provide an initial insight for your teams that works with your teams' culture. You may wish to provide this level of training to your advocates, to the people who you want to lead practices in meetings, or work with smaller teams on their introduction of mindfulness. I would suggest you explore the types of training that are available and find something that works for your teams.

Review

We also revisited the subject a year later. At another team event, I delivered a short presentation about mindfulness and how we had applied it in the programme to date, and led the whole team in a three-minute practice. This was important for a number of reasons. It explained the mindfulness ethos to the team, that very largely comprised of new people. But we also wanted to demonstrate continuity for those who had been with us from the start and make sure that everyone heard consistent messages about what we were trying to achieve by being a mindful programme.

Achieve sustainability

I will mention this a few times throughout the book, because there is little point in going to all this effort and getting all these benefits for the organisation, if you see them melt away the moment you step away from the place. As my time with the programme came to an end, I became aware that the sustainability of the mindful culture could be at risk with my departure. This may well have been remarkable arrogance on my part, but I was the instigator of the approach and the only person leading practices. I invited people to self-nominate for mindfulness training sessions and I led those sessions. This was the start of something that could have been equivalent to the "training the trainer" approach.

When I look back at that programme, I am really pleased that we got as far as we did, but I think we could have gone so much further. Whilst we reaped significant benefits, we simply did not maximise the benefit of the approach.

7 How to implement organisational mindfulness: how do you normally eat your elephants?

If you are now thinking that mindfulness might be right for your organisation, how do you achieve that culture change? I love the rather cheesy expression, "culture eats strategy for breakfast". To me, this emphasises just how tough it can be to shift a culture, but equally how powerful the culture of an organisation is. If we can get this fundamental background or canvas right, then we can paint the picture we want.

There are a number of challenges with culture change. First, it is a change! This is self-evident, but it is remarkable how resistant to change we can be. Even a change that many people would assume would be positive, like getting a new car or going on holiday, can be intensely stressful. If you consider how much time people spend at work and how familiar they get with the way things are, the way things are done, then it may not be surprising that when you suggest that something could be improved, the people resist, especially when they helped to co-create the current set-up. This is hard enough to achieve with something that is nowadays fairly routine, like an IT upgrade. But in this instance, you are asking people to work differently and even approach their thoughts differently! So, it is a potentially hard sell. You are potentially straying into territory that people feel has nothing to do with work. What could be more personal than the way our minds work?

The other issue I'd suggest is that it may look to you to be impossible. The scale of the challenge of getting the whole place to behave differently is just overwhelming. So don't! Most cultural changes to organisations that I have experienced (though not all) have been incremental. So rather than looking to suddenly win everyone over, maybe look at the effect you can achieve in a small area of the organisation. Maybe with some team members that you think are likely to be supportive. These people may become your advocates.

Another thing you may want to consider is that change happens all the time. Change to the culture may feel like it is at the margins and the core values are retained, but all organisations that last any length of time will go through changes as people join and leave the team and perhaps the team shrinks and grows. So, you are not working in a vacuum. You are not trying to fight or move a single solid edifice. Organisations are much more fluid than that, however immutable they may seem.

Also consider what you mean by culture change. There may be many aspects of the way people already work that you do not want to lose. You may want to retain the high risk-taking attitude of some of the executives, or the fast pace of the shop floor. We are more likely to be successful if we are enhancing what people already admire about the place. Taking high risks then, after reflecting for a few seconds, might avoid some losses. The high-paced shop floor may be safer, if people are wholly present as they move around it.

But having said all that, let's accept that change is generally hard. So, where do you start?

Can you identify some activities your organisation already does that could be generating shared attention? If so, can you identify any that people already admire, but feel could be improved? The best bet might be to build on what you already have.

How you are perceived also plays a role in your success. If you are seen as imposing something that you like, over and above what others think is the way things should or always have been done, this is likely to result in resentment, even if you are right in the long run. It may make achieving your objectives far harder. Take a moment and see if there are some people who might be interested in trying this in their area and maybe see how they want to build the ideas of mindfulness into their activities.

There is something here too about not always knowing the answers. This may well just be me, but I am totally capable of deciding how a thing should turn out, how it should look or operate. Apart from demonstrating that I am a mindful control freak … the point of mentioning this is that as a sense of maximum control is really valuable when embarking on a construction project, for example, and whilst you will want to have a plan and you will want to have clear and agreed objectives, you have the luxury of being able to iterate here. You may be able to learn from your potential advocates, as you go along. What is more, if you start this process with a willingness to let things emerge from the people with whom you are working, they are more likely to own and enjoy the final outcome, than a process that you have imposed.

Another challenge is that, whilst personal mindfulness practice is less novel than it was even five years ago, organisational mindfulness is still (I believe) quite new. Like any new approach or idea, it may come across as radical and untested and therefore a risk. What's more, regardless of what other organisations have done, it hasn't been applied in yours and you want the process of application to be creative, so you don't actually know the detail of the final design. This presents both a risk and an opportunity. On the one hand when people say, this is untested and risky, they are in part right. But then you can be upfront and say that you want to work with people to examine how this will work in your organisation so that people can own the change.

You also have the advantage of the research that tells us mindfulness is a positive thing that develops benefits and that this change applies the same principles to organisations.

So, in answer to the question, "how do you eat your elephant?", maybe the standard answer of "in individual bites" does still work. But perhaps you don't actually want to eat it. Maybe you want to keep the elephant, but encourage it to walk in a different direction, or in a different way. Still a daunting prospect, but perhaps less daunting than eating an entire elephant.

It may also be worth going back to the idea of starting small, whilst being ambitious. Thinking again of a relatively small part of the business, with potential allies to begin with, may be an idea. This might be enough to encourage your elephant to follow your lead … *Enough with the elephants.*

So, if you are trying to achieve incremental change, my suggestion would be to look at:

- Processes
- Products
- People

Processes

By processes, I mean any activity or set-piece event undertaken by your organisation. This could be a management meeting, it could be an all-staff event. It could be weekly or monthly financial reporting, risk management activities. It could be weekly newsletters, mailshots to customers, advertising campaign developments. Big or small, there will be a huge number of activities that are routinely undertaken. Maybe pick five of these processes and consider the question: "have they become so routine that it is hard for people in your team to bring their full attention to what is happening?".

You may want to pick five really influential processes, or you may want to start small, considering that you want to experiment safely with this change. It is important to consider what is right for you and your organisation. The great thing about jumping in at the deep end is you make a big impact and it can shake things up quickly. But you don't want key processes to fail and your mindfulness approach to be blamed. So, if you want to go large, make sure all the people involved are onside and are clear on what is changing and how to make it work. The great thing about a piloting approach is you get to test your thinking, but it is less likely to be noticed and you may lose momentum. Also, having got the buy-in to try this, people may not have the patience to wait for a second phase. You will be best placed to decide which way to go, but you may want to test your thinking with a trusted colleague.

Once you have your processes, what do you do with them? You are likely to have some people who "own" the process. They may be the expert in that part of the organisation's activity or they may just have been doing it a long time. It may be that they are different from the people who operate the process. But, remembering the idea that you want people to own the change, rather than trying to impose a new way of working, perhaps test with that process owner and person or people who run the process what they find frustrating about it. Why is it hard to bring their full attention to it? Is it dull, just boring, or is it not recognised as being vital? Is it repetitive or is it too complex, so it is hard to follow? If you are changing the processes for which you are responsible, then ask these questions of yourself.

Also, consider whether the people you are talking to are quite happy with the way it is; if so, how might you help them to see that it could be enhanced? Maybe even challenge the status quo by asking, would it help if the process were improved to make it easier for you to bring your attention to what's going on? If the answer is yes, then work with them to see how the process can be tweaked to help with this.

To quote Sir David Brailsford CBE, the former Performance Director of British Cycling, when describing his approach to marginal gains: "The whole principle came from the idea that if you broke down everything you could think of that goes into riding a bike, and then improve it by 1 per cent, you will get a significant increase when you put them all together." In the spirit of the British Cycling team, you may be looking for the accumulation of many marginal improvements, to achieve your revolution.

So, you may be looking at just having five three-minute breathing practices during the day, or you might consider changing the colour of the forms that are being used, so they are more interesting. You may be looking at rotating the responsibilities among the team, so the activity is slightly fresher for each person in the team. You may be offering the individual some mindfulness training. Whatever change we are making we are trying, with the person who performs the process, to help support them and their colleagues to be more mindful in what they are doing. To better attend to the process.

Maybe try the changes for a week, working out a feedback form before and after the change to see if things have changed for the better for the individual. If they have, you know you are onto something. If they haven't, then dig a bit deeper, this is new territory, it probably shouldn't go perfectly every time we try something new. See what alternative changes might work instead. Did you both miss something in your design? Feel free to iterate; try and have some fun with it.

Once you have changed the process, document it. Make sure you take credit and capture the positive impact that has been achieved. This is the start of your evidence base either for bigger things, or just to keep going and to defend this approach from the cynics.

Don't just capture the feedback from the process change though. Try and capture lessons learned from the way you have introduced the change. Your timing might have been off. Your introduction to the subject could have been more accessible? Whatever the feedback, it can help you for the next process or to improve how this change is perceived. People are more likely to accept perceived mistakes in the introduction of a change, if the mistake is going to be learned from.

As you are working with the process owner, I'd suggest you emphasise that you are aiming to improve the success of the process. So, this is business focussed, practical and aimed at supporting the outcomes of the business. This helps because it works against the misconception around mindfulness that it is solely valuable in improving well-being. It may also be the case that the process owner has been frustrated by the fact that the process has never worked effectively and that this has become the opportunity, the excuse, to make changes and thereby improve outcomes.

I worked in programme assurance for many years. This largely involved talking to people who were delivering large and challenging programmes and testing whether delivery was on track. I would look at documents and interview people who were involved in the business and affected by the project. The challenges faced by the programme leaders often quickly became apparent. Interestingly, when I got to speak to the programme leaders, the approach to my questions could vary considerably. Sometimes people were understandably defensive and tried to explain why things were not as they should be. But quite often, the people that I spoke to welcomed the fact that they had someone they could talk to, to explain their own frustration at the position in which they found themselves. It could almost become a counselling session, where the programme leaders poured out their hearts and hoped that I could provide some kind of support. In practical terms, these were the most effective conversations. I was always much more convinced by someone who was open about why things were not as they should be, than by those who either tried to claim that everything was fine, or attempted to justify the position of a challenged programme. You may find the same with your process owner. They may be genuinely grateful that you are taking the time to talk to them about a problem they have faced for some considerable time. The fact that you are trying to bring mindfulness into the mix, may not be that relevant to them. What you are actually doing is paying them some attention and bringing some corporate attention to something that has needed fixing.

If you then move on with some success and lessons behind you to the next process, you are by stealth introducing mindfulness into the very core of the organisation. At a fundamental process level, people are behaving differently and seeing the benefits of a mindful approach.

Worked example

I'm going to use the example of programme reporting because it is close to my heart. This is an incredibly difficult process to get right and yet, on the face of it, it should be incredibly easy. All you are doing is gathering data from the different parts of a programme. You are then combining that data into a report, which then goes to more senior people, often the programme board or the senior responsible owner (SRO) who is accountable for the delivery of the programme.

Where it gets complicated is that (as for the rest of the programme) it is affected by time, cost and quality and, above all, does not happen in a vacuum; oh, and then there's judgment.

The people who are reporting their data often want to put the best spin on things. They do not want to tell anyone where things are not going to plan. This is normally completely the wrong strategy, as it stores up problems further down the line, and prevents anyone from actually helping them. When it comes to light that there is an issue, which it almost always does, it doesn't make the person responsible for embellishing the truth look great either ... however, it happens. So, you have people who are telling you part of the truth.

They also tell you late. I have always wanted to focus on delivery, rather than reporting. Again, perfectly natural. The people involved in delivering the programme are grown-ups and doing a thing that they are qualified to do, so instinctively there is resistance to reporting to another grown-up on what they are doing. This is exacerbated by the knowledge that it is, in turn, going to be reported to a more senior grown-up. It just feels like bureaucracy and when it's done badly, that can be pretty much all it is. But when it is done well, it can save an enormous amount of time, effort and money and help the people who are doing the reporting. But the bottom line is, people miss their deadlines, routinely. This means that whoever is compiling the report has less time to test the content, make amendments and get it into a fit state for the boss.

And then there is quality. Responsibility for reporting is often handed to people who do not understand its importance or how it works or indeed the data that is being sent forward. So, there are also often issues with quality standards and compliance.

The point about not operating in a vacuum is simply that the report normally has to be produced on the same day as about a thousand other things and you are reporting on a moving target – you don't actually ever have a fully up-to date-report. If the project is moving forward, the time that it takes to actually produce the report is time during which the data is becoming obsolete.

And then the judgement comes in when you have to consider how information can usefully be presented. If you are doing your job properly, you need to be transparent about the situation and cut through the spinning of the teams. But in most programme reports, the author has a summary section and there is also something about how you choose to say X things have not been delivered and the team have developed a plan to get it back on track. You can simply say that and leave it at that. Or you can say that X things have not been delivered, but that the team have shown you a plan to recover the position and also whether you think the plan is realistic. So, you can use your role as the arbiter of the truth to signal to the SRO how urgent the matter is and how much of their attention they need to bring to this programme at this stage. (For me, this is further evidence that programme management is a mindful practice, but you've probably guessed that.)

How can you introduce mindfulness into the reporting process and thereby try and address some of these challenges? One simple thought might be to hold a meeting with all the contributors, or even better, those accountable for the data in the report, before the report is submitted. It doesn't have to be a long meeting, but you suddenly have everyone who owns part of the report in a meeting about the report. They may not even know that their section has not yet been submitted. But, after the first time when their page is blank (in my experience) they will be more likely to make certain that it is completed before the meeting next time. The fact that people are being required to consider the report collectively also has the impact of making people think differently about the act of reporting. It is less someone else's problem and now has become more of a shared priority. Also, all of the data owners will see their data in situ, next to the data of the other data owners. This is likely to help with quality for future reporting cycles.

The timing of this meeting can also help with accuracy. It gives people a final chance to update on recent changes or events. On judgment, it makes this a bit harder and the data owners are going to see what you have said in advance of it going to the boss. But this is a good discipline for you. You need to be sure you can defend what you are saying and also, and even more powerfully, it gives the people on whom you are reporting a chance to challenge you and appreciate why you are saying it. This may require a bit more resilience, but actually it can help avoid difficult and broken relationships, when challenging messages have to be given and it can actually lead to an increase in respect in those relationships.

I am not suggesting mindfulness intrinsically needs more meetings. Meetings have often been the bane of my professional life. But I am suggesting that a change to a process that requires the key people responsible for a process to bring their attention together, as well as share responsibility, could lead to an improvement in the products and outcomes resulting from that process. I'd also suggest that if you are explicit about why this is necessary, it will be more likely to happen and more likely to achieve the desired outcome. It may be advisable not to lead with the suggestion that "as a reporting group we need to be more mindful". I think this leaves you open to challenge and possibly to losing your audience. But if you explain that you want to "share updates from across the programme with all the reporting leads and achieve a joint review of the report before it goes to the board" then you may be more likely to have people show up. It would be a brave work strand or project lead who, when offered the opportunity to review something about their area of responsibility before it goes the board, decides to leave that to their peers. However you try and describe it, what you are achieving is a moment of shared attention: on this occasion this shared attention is focussed on your report.

Products

It was definitely Paolo who opened my eyes to the value of this thinking: the fact that the very reports we develop can have the opposite effect to the one we are aiming for. Rather than stimulating discussion and debate, they can stifle conversation; rather than achieving a shared point of attention, they can distract from the key messages. The reports we produce can, by their very design, lead to people switching off. This is, I am sure, not just true of project and programme management paperwork. What about end-of-year staff appraisals? Accident reports? Food hygiene reports? Planning applications? Any number of pieces of paperwork that are intended to provoke a response and some action actually drive us to the edge of somnambulism!

When I was taught by Paolo, we were invited to design a reporting tool, that would provoke discussion, or achieve shared attention. Because I had been banging on about mindfulness all week, one or my colleagues came up with the idea of designing a report based on a mandala. It may have looked unconventional and not been in corporate colours, but it would have been hard to ignore!

Now, going back to the principles of incremental change and marginal gains which underlie this book it may be a step too far to ask your board to consider data presented on a wall in a pattern of psychedelic swirls. But, why not establish with the process owner what would work? Not every form has to be a square table with rows of conventional data. There is a reason that PowerPoint has such a plethora of styles for presentations and why CV designers charge small fortunes to help you make your CV stand out. We are aiming to do something similar, but rather than just grabbing attention and standing out as being different, we are after something else, we are after shared attention, shared mindfulness.

What we are looking for is something that draws the reader in and makes them think about the subject, the detail and enables a group of people to have an informed conversation about the issue at hand. We also have to be realistic about what our organisation's culture will tolerate. But my suggestion would be –be bold! You may be surprised how willing people are to try something new and then to adopt it and ask others to replicate it, if it works! But one route that I have previously used successfully is to build some options. So, look at the date when you are aiming to present and then try presenting it in a range of styles. Then opt for two or three designs that you think will generate shared attention. I will discuss how you might want to approach this later, but again you may not choose to call this mindfulness. You may just be redesigning your products and then suggesting that your options are an improvement to the way that you present your data and that you would like input on which, if any, are preferred. When I did this at one large organisation, the most radical solution won out straight away.

Worked example

To try and demonstrate what I have in mind, I have set out below some ideas for how you might want to redesign the products you have already. I have made up the initial example and tried not to make it too dull. I have then created an alternative solution. You may feel that you would not want to try the alternative, which is absolutely fine. I'm not suggesting this particular alternative is one you would want to adopt, it's just to explore the idea of how you might want to creatively use your products to generate shared attention.

I have used a programme highlight report, to keep to the reporting theme.

Original

Project Future IT	Reporting period Jan '20

The project has made a significant step forward having completed negotiations with a supplier and finalised a contract. The planning position has improved dramatically with the implementation plan now complete. It will be presented to the programme board for approval in February. The resourcing position has also significantly improved following the appointment of three project managers, although the first of these will only join in one month and the other two will come on stream over three months.

Time remains tight to achieve the original completion date of October '20. However, all of the top three risks reported last month have been significantly mitigated.

Key achievements previous period		Key achievements next period	
02-Jan	Contract finalised	05-Feb	Communication plan to launch
10-Jan	Three project managers recruited	10-Feb	Whole-team event
25-Jan	Plan for implementation completed	22- Feb	Pilot roll-out starts

Risk assessment			
	Risk definition	Previous risk assessment	Current risk assessment
Risk No 1	Delays to planning cause implementation to slip	Red	Amber
Risk No 2	Resourcing constraints will delay implementation	Red	Amber
Risk No 3	Staff do not engage with the new IT system	Amber	Amber

This looks to me as if the project was in a tricky situation last month. The risk assessments were challenging and they have all improved. What do you want your board to focus on? There is something here about a heroic achievement by the team. My experience suggests they would have got a bit of a hammering at the last board. So, how have they gone from no contract, no plan and no people, to contract finalised, plan in place and up for approval and people on their way? Apart from celebrating the fact that more project managers are coming on board, you may want the board members to consider what has gone well and who is responsible. Are there any lessons learned that could be replicated in other parts of the business? But also, is the plan realistic?

Has it been rushed and likewise what about the people who have been recruited? The board will hopefully know about the contract, as someone senior should have signed it off, but does the whole board know who your suppliers are and why they were appointed? Also, what is next? Is the board going to be asked to speak at the whole-team event? How do the people in the business feel about the project? There was clearly a risk recently that they were not engaging. So, lots to bring their attention to.

Possible option 2

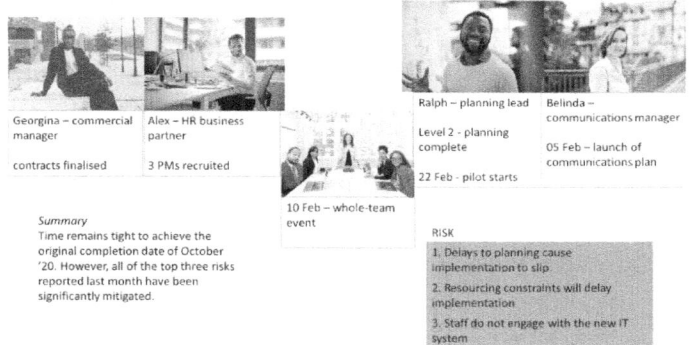

Georgina – commercial manager
Alex – HR business partner
Ralph – planning lead
Belinda – communications manager

contracts finalised
3 PMs recruited
Level 2 - planning complete
05 Feb – launch of communications plan

22 Feb - pilot starts

10 Feb – whole-team event

Summary
Time remains tight to achieve the original completion date of October '20. However, all of the top three risks reported last month have been significantly mitigated.

RISK
1. Delays to planning cause implementation to slip
2. Resourcing constraints will delay implementation
3. Staff do not engage with the new IT system

As already mentioned, the subsequent design may not be right for your organisation. You may also think that the original scenario is not realistic, or that you have far more sophisticated data on your existing reporting. All of these may be fair observations, but I am just exploring whether the alternative solution provides an option that is more likely to engender shared attention by your board.

To me, the aesthetics alone are more inviting. The original table format, with regular boxes and totally detached data, tells me very little and frankly looks like a very simple version of almost every report I have ever read. On one level, that's not a bad thing. I know where to look for the information. I get the impression that it is put forward by someone who understands planning and risk. But it is boring. And if I have back-to-back meetings from 8 a.m. to 6 p.m. then I am now trying to prepare for the board the night before the meeting. It takes a considerable amount of energy, after I have said goodnight to the kids, to bring myself to look at something that is dull! The circles with people's faces and the flows of data are, if nothing else, interesting to my eye. They kind of draw me in. I know Georgina. I gave her a hard time at the last board because they were so far behind, but she's got it back on track, fair play.

The experience of reading the alternative report is in itself more engaging. I have a more human connection to the information, with pictures of people and movement in the design. I am starting to feel something as I read it, rather than just sitting in my executive head, trying to rationalise the data.

To a mindfulness coach, this sounds like I am moving from a very conceptual place to a more perceptual place. I am starting to more fully and physically connect with the information, with the programme and the people involved.

In turn, I feel more likely to be able to bring my experience to problems posed by the data. I now have a more human connection with Georgina. I am more likely to engage in her story and therefore in this programme. The images of the people remind me that the IT implementation will have a huge impact on the people in the organisation. As a board member, I have always believed it when we have collectively said that the staff are the organisation. But when I'm looking at board papers at 9 p.m. after a full day, it is easy to see the IT project as something that is being done to the business without any connection to the people. In looking at the alternative design, I am being required to connect viscerally with the people who will be affected and who I have said "are the organisation". I am being required to pay attention to this data, because I am starting to feel that it matters to real people.

People

This may be the hardest part of bringing mindfulness into the heart of your organisation. Even though existing processes and products may have their advocates, they are not people. Despite some folk having an emotional attachment to the way something has been done, if you can demonstrate that the changes deliver a functional improvement, then it's hard to oppose. People are a whole different issue.

My experience has been that in fact many people are really interested and keen. But there is also often still a significant degree of scepticism and lack of understanding. People may also think that they are here to work and don't need to be told by someone how they should do this work. Especially if they have been doing it quite successfully for years! They may also have some significant and very justifiable resistance to ideas like mindfulness. As we have explored, many people may make associations with religion but regardless of that, this is about how our minds work and there can be little that is more personal than that.

Another perfectly understandable resistance that you may encounter is from people who do not want to 'improve' or 'be improved'. The last two areas we explored were about improving inanimate processes or products. Now we are asking people to improve the ways they work: in essence, themselves.

There are many reasons to push back against a mindful approach. What is wrong with the way I am at the moment? No one has suggested I am not doing a good job already. Who are you to tell me how to think? This stuff is all very well for people who are under stress or suffer from mental illness, but I don't, I'm fine, so I don't need this. I come here to do a job, I don't need to be psychoanalysed or made to feel that I should do something differently to avoid stress or improve, when I am not stressed and I do a good job. You are just trying to get me to work harder for no more pay.

I am sure there are many more reasons. But none of these responses need to put us off. They are just not the basis of why we are offering these tools and also, it is worth remembering, this stuff is voluntary. But let's address these concerns. The approach taken by all accredited mindfulness teachers should be that secular mindfulness is just that. It is not a gateway to any religion or sect. It is a set of tools to help a person manage their minds differently. Most trainers will not pretend that this stuff is new and will be explicit that it has its roots in a 2,500-year-old tradition. There may be connections to Buddhism, but many teachers are also happy to point out that most major religions have a tradition of meditation, so this is not about religion and certainly not about God. This is about some very practical techniques that a person may find helpful. As it has nothing to do with God, it is certainly not an alternative to prayer and should not be seen as such.

With regard to performance, these techniques are all about helping people to thrive, both in their workplace and their whole lives. This could be something that we already do, in which case, great, but you may find these ideas hep you to continue to thrive.

Above all, I would suggest these techniques are voluntary. No one should be trying to require team members to take part. If, for any reason, someone is uncomfortable with mindfulness, then that's absolutely fine. Again, we need to make sure that the use of mindfulness techniques does not become something that is used to exclude those who do not wish to take part. These are just some helpful tools. Not a stick with which to beat people. This is really important.

There is also a significant ethical point that I would like to flag here. There is a risk that some organisations (probably those that hang onto the "lunch is for wimps" culture) look at mindfulness as a way of getting more out of their staff. If that is your ambition, please think again. First, it won't work and second, I feel it is unethical.

It is my experience that I am able to endure more, as a result of my mindfulness practice. When I first came across mindfulness, my life was a mess and I was not coping with the pressures of an upper middle-management job. Within five years of applying mindfulness techniques, I had been promoted twice to a director position on a programme of national importance. The scale and intensity of the pressure was unprecedented in my experience. But I was able to cope. There were bumpy bits – I'm not pretending that there weren't! But I coped.

So, I had gone from not being able to cope in an intense environment, to being able to thrive in an enormously difficult environment and a significant change had been the tools presented by mindfulness. But the reality is that part of being able to cope was knowing when to step away. If I hadn't, then it would have reached a point at which it was not sustainable. My suggestion as to why exploiting mindfulness in this way will not work is that your staff will still fall over. They will just do so harder, later!

Why is it unethical? I believe because, at its heart, mindfulness has compassion. Whilst much of this book is focussed on the idea that mindfulness can improve more than just well-being, it is not compassionate or sustainable to use these techniques to wring every last ounce of endeavour out of people.

Mindfulness can enhance people's capacity to endure highly intense situations. It has done so for me. For a short period of time, this can be great for the individual and for the organisation; but push this too far and you will just be storing up problems for both. You will also not be achieving the ambition of organisational mindfulness. Whilst part of your organisation (some individuals) will be applying mindfulness techniques, they will not be supported by the ethos of the organisation. In turn this will mean that you will miss out on the prize of a genuinely mindful organisation.

But applying mindfulness ethically will, I have no doubt, enable your people to achieve more individually and collectively as well as to thrive under pressure. It will just mean that you are not using mindfulness as a way of wringing the last ounce of energy out of them.

If we are clear that this stuff is not about requiring a person to change their opinions and doesn't need to threaten anyone's beliefs – if we try and make it clear that mindfulness is purely a toolkit that some people may choose to adopt to help them with their tasks and to look after themselves and, above all, that it is optional – then we may have a bit less push-back.

Another barrier to entry may be the word "mindfulness". Most of this book is about trying to demonstrate that mindfulness is practical, pragmatic and not about hippies and joss sticks. But unfortunately, there have been too many situation comedy references and negative newspaper articles for some of the stereotypes to be easily dismissed. This can be particularly challenging when trying to secure funding in sectors where there is a threat that the media will challenge spending on new ideas, which is of course unfortunate when mindfulness is very likely to improve performance, including reducing absenteeism. But regardless of the merits or not of the public perception of mindfulness, you may feel we have not got far enough with a public level of understanding to use this term in your organisation.

I have heard the same approach described as mind fitness, well-being or resilience training. Really, as a pragmatist, I don't think what you call it matters as much as what it is that you are actually implementing and how well you implement it. Consider then what will work for you, but if you do call your mindfulness techniques by a different name, don't be surprised if people say "this is very much like mindfulness".

It is also right that whilst I wouldn't encourage people to be underhand or deceptive (in fact I would caution against it on the grounds that you may be caught out and this might undermine your overall approach), you may feel that it is necessary to start to introduce some of these incremental changes by stealth. For the first two categories, you are in essence improving processes and products. Whilst you might explain that you are hoping that the changed approach will make it easier for people to do their jobs, or process the data, you don't even have to say the word "mindfulness".

Bringing these techniques into the daily lives of people by stealth may be a bit harder. But even saying that, there is much that can be explained without using the word "mindfulness," if that is really going to be a barrier to people gaining the benefits of mindfulness techniques.

If you are going to adopt a fully open approach, then my suggestion would be to introduce the idea of mindfulness at team events. You may find it easier to get external speakers to introduce the idea, to overcome the barrier of people seeing you as a mindfulness instructor or teacher. A good external speaker has the advantage of being able to answer challenges or lead groups without it having an impact on their personal standing and they also have the kudos of being known from the start as a trainer and "expert," not as a member of the existing team. But I would strongly encourage you to choose your speaker well. It is important that they are credible for your team. There are many amazing mindfulness trainers available, but not all of them have experience of working in a corporate environment and not all of them will be able to speak convincingly of the challenges faced in a workplace like yours. If you are trying to win hearts and minds in your work environment, I'd suggest you need a person who can tell a convincing story as well as lead a group in a mindfulness practice.

Once you have introduced your group to the concepts of mindfulness and gauged their reaction, there may be a number of ways to bring mindfulness into the lives of the people in your team. The classic way would be to offer mindfulness training. This can be done in groups to manage the cost and there are a number of suppliers in the UK who can build a training package that will meet your needs, but again I would suggest that it is essential you select an accredited trainer and that your trainer should be credible for your audience.

If your mindfulness approach is going to be sustained, you may want to have mindfulness champions within your organisation. These individuals are likely to be the people who were the most responsive and keen when mindfulness was mentioned. They may need some more or different training than the majority of the people in your organisation, but they are the ones who will be able to provide training for new joiners. They will also be the people who stay connected to mindfulness networks outside the organisation, stay in touch with developments in the mindfulness community and champion the ongoing importance of mindfulness to your organisation, after the initial (hopefully) enthusiasm has subsided.

One of the key differences between organisational mindfulness and just training some people to have a mindfulness practice, is that the organisation actively supports people in their mindfulness practice and that the ways of working of the organisation supports personal practice as well. You may want to consider setting up lunchtime-led practices; these can be just 20 minutes long, but can make sure people have somewhere to go to expand their practice and share experiences with other practitioners. You may want to include reference to mindfulness in the organisation's newsletter, so that the language just becomes a bit more familiar and a bit less odd. You may want to run some stories from people within the organisation who have found it helpful, to demonstrate that it is having a positive impact and encourage those who have not engaged with the idea so far to give it a go.

As part of this training or communications strategy, you may want to introduce small, practical examples of mindfulness in action that anyone can apply, whether or not they have been on the training, and something that they can do at their desk, as well as with a group of colleagues.

Worked example

You could run an item in your newsletter inviting people to try and do a three-minute practice at their desks when they first get in from their commute. So, maybe an article in your newsletter, like the one below:

"Hi all, Andrew here. You will hopefully now be used to me mentioning mindfulness following our training programme. I thought I would remind you of one of the ideas that the trainer introduced and that I have found really quick and helpful. The three-minute practice.

I find my commute into work pretty stressful and so by the time I've got to my desk in the morning I am often pretty cross and still thinking about the person who barged in front of me in the queue for the bus, or alternatively I'm already stressing about the 72 emails that have mysteriously appeared since last night. So, I've started to do the three-minute practice at my desk, just before I start the day. So far no one has noticed, or if they have then they are too polite to say anything. This is all I do:

I make sure I am sitting comfortably with a fairly straight back and that my head is comfortable. I don't normally close my eyes as I feel a bit self-conscious, so I just lower my gaze.
Then I just notice the support of the chair and my feet on the floor. I notice the temperature in the room and any sounds outside or inside the room.

After about 15 seconds, I bring my attention to my breath, the changes that each breath makes to my body, so movement in my back or my shoulders. I keep my attention there for about 40 seconds and if my mind wanders, I just gently bring my attention back to the breath.

The I bring my attention to the in-breath. The very start of the breath and I notice the temperature of the air and where I sense it, maybe in the throat or the tip of the nose or upper lip.

Then, after another 40 seconds, I move my attention to the out-breath and the very end of the breath, before the next in-breath. Again, I look out for what I notice about the temperature and where I sense it.
After 40 seconds, I broaden my attention and notice again all the movement from the whole breath, in my shoulders and back, for example.

Then, after 40 more seconds, I broaden my attention still further to noticing the support of the chair, my feet on the floor, the temperature in the room and any sounds inside and outside the room and then I wiggle my fingers or toes and raise my gaze.

Less than three minutes and I have left my journey in behind me and I am properly present, and able to face the now 74 emails ...

Maybe give it a go and let me know how you get on. If you'd like to practise that practice with others, we'll have a version of this practice led for us, at the mindfulness drop-in on Thursday.

Have a great day.
Andrew"

Again, you may not like the style and Thursdays may not be the best day for you to have a mindfulness drop-in. But that's not the point. The purpose is to offer a suggestion. How can you make mindfulness in your workplace structurally, culturally normalised and supported? How can you start to help your people get on board with your mindfulness approach? Communication, training, coaching and leading by example will be key.

8   More about implementation: a bit of programme management

With my project and programme management background, I would say the next bit, wouldn't I? So far, we have understood the idea of mindfulness, we have developed a vision (the four-quadrant model), we have started to break down the areas of the organisation we want to affect into processes, products and people. But we haven't worked out how to implement the change. This chapter looks at how you might go about getting the support of your peers or leaders and planning to make the vision a reality.

Suggestion 1: Be clear about why you are doing this

The quadrant model is a good start for describing what a mindful organisation might look like, but you have to be clear on why you are doing this and what is your vision. The chances are that delivering this will be quite hard at times and may require additional work for which you are not being paid. It is important, then, to cling on to the why, for the times when the "what the heck?" is all that's in your head.

If your aim is to improve the well-being of people in the team, that is great and there may be nothing wrong with that approach. Similarly, if your ambition is to get your team to be more accurate, resilient or creative, that is also fine. You may want to consider the culture of where you are working and establish what the most credible approach might be. If you are working in a place that has a strong profit motive, then having a vision that aligns to at least some extent with the prevailing culture of the organisation may resonate more strongly with the people you are hoping will join in, and may help win over any bosses that you need onside. You will be facing enough challenges, so working out what will support the organisation to achieve its objectives may be prudent. This doesn't just apply in a profit-driven organisation. If collaboration or support are the watchwords of your business, talking exclusively about resilience and delivery, may not win you the backing you need.

A key thing for me, is that just because mindfulness seems to be in vogue at the moment, probably shouldn't be sufficient reason to start this. It will not be sustained and may actually undermine your chance to make a real change in your organisation. I'd suggest being clear in your own mind about the reasons you want to do this is a great first place to start, because then when you are talking to others about your ideas, they will quickly see there is more behind this than current trends.

Suggestion 2: What are the costs and benefits?

Many projects are started without clear benefits and with no way of measuring them. That need not be the case with this work. Some of the benefits may be "soft" so how are you actually going to measure the whole organisation's ability to concentrate? But, I invite all the people I train to complete a short questionnaire before and after the training, to track whether it is delivering any change. You may wish to repeat the questionnaire after 6 and 12 months, but with the caveat that you will want to know whether the people you are asking have maintained their mindfulness practice. Don't let the results of your hard work be slanted by the fact people haven't made the most of the opportunity that you have presented.

That said, of course, knowing how many people have kept the practice going is an important test of whether the initial training stuck and whether the structural elements of your programme are having the desired, sustained impact.

There may be "harder" benefits that you can track, for example a reduction in the number of sick days taken

Cost for any project is always tricky. People should be concerned about where they are investing their money and being clear on the actual cost can help with confidence.

Decide whether you need external support. You may feel that you are confident in your own practice to deliver the required training, or you may feel that external people who have experience of training mindfulness in businesses, would be helpful. There are numerous organisations now providing mindfulness training. Make sure that, where national accreditation systems exist, the organisations you approach are accredited and that the trainers they supply will be accredited.

There are not as yet many organisations that support the type of structural change I am advocating. So, you may need to do most of this design yourself. But the whole point of the structural approach is to support personal practice and sustain the change, so this work should be well worthwhile.

- Have a clear vision of why you want to do this:
    - *to improve the well-being of the team, improve people's ability to concentrate and reduce sick absence*

- Understand what "this" is:
  - *70% of the team take part in some type of training in mindfulness practices, weekly mindfulness drop-in sessions are established and team meetings routinely start with a three-minute practice*

- Establish ideas on how to achieve "this":
  - *event for the team to hear the proposition, be introduced to mindfulness and agree a mindful code of conduct; some external trainers to provide training and some evaluation*

Once you have done this work, it should be possible to build a picture of cost. Don't forget hidden costs. In the example above, you have the cost of the event, the time people aren't working because they are at the event, the cost of the external trainers, the cost of the people attending the training, the cost of the time spent conducting the evaluation, and so on. But if you bring these costs together openly, it will demonstrate your candour and thoroughness.

In terms of benefit, you may not have to save too many sick absence days before you have more than offset the cost you are recommending.

But, in essence, before you start you should know how much you are going to spend and when, and what are the benefits you are going to deliver and when. If you set this out clearly at the start it will demonstrate that you are serious about what will be achieved and that you have a plan to measure both the rate at which money is being spent and the rate at which the benefits are, or are not, being delivered.

Suggestion 3: Don't be afraid to test your thinking

Test your vision. This may all seem self-evident to you. But are you alone in this? You may be surprised how many people are interested and supportive, but if you spring on people a fully formed vision of the mindful future as you see it, you may have lost sight already of the third quadrant in the model, being mindful of each other. We need to consider how other people feel. There may be many reasons why people do not support your vision, so test it and see whether you can build a consensus around it. That process may fundamentally change your own approach.

It is entirely possible, in our enthusiasm to create a complete view of how things should proceed, to forget that we are dealing with people, so my suggestion would be to invite some colleagues you trust to act a sounding board, get some other people's views on your ideas and be willing to adapt the plan.

Suggestion 4: Write a business case

This does not have to be War and Peace, but having a simple, accessible document that sets out why you are doing this, what the possible benefits are, what the cost is likely to be and how it will be achieved, is a strong discipline. It will require you to consider these questions for yourself as well as put all the answers to your peers' or more senior colleagues' questions in one place. It also significantly enhances your credibility if you have already bothered to do this, before you are asked for it.

For major projects, the writing of business cases can easily become a small industry in itself. But, essentially, even for the largest project they should just set out: why is the thing worth doing, how much will it cost, what will the benefits be (and how will they be measured), what governance will exist around the delivery and how will the project be achieved. You are not trying to deliver High Speed 2! You are trying to introduce some mindfulness to your organisation. So be proportionate, put what you need to into your business case and leave it at that. Another top tip is that the people who have to read business cases never have time to read business cases, so the more concise you can be, whilst providing all the information required, will be much appreciated.

Even if it is never read by anyone else, this document will have done its job. It will have given you a chance to get your thinking straight: test your ideas, work out the cost and how you will measure the benefits. And if you haven't written it at the start, my experience is someone will ask for it when you least expect it and when you don't have time to write it.

Suggestion 5: Plan

Planning is essential to success. And as soon as you start to plan, you may have the same experience that I always have, that is you will immediately see that you need more time than you expected. Taking the time to develop a realistic plan can help you understand the resources you need to deliver mindfulness training, when you need them, who you are dependent on for their part in this delivery and how long they will take. For example, if you are intending to provide some formal mindfulness training, are you intending to buy the services of some trainers? How long does your procurement process take? This may depend on the value of the contract. Do you have rooms available, where the training can take place? How far in advance do you have to book the rooms? Do you have a budget and can you approve the spend, or do you need to get approval? If you do need approval, how long does that take? And so on.

One method that I've used is to set aside some time to think of all the activities you need do and to write them up on post-its with the duration of the activities written on each note. If they have to happen in sequence, you can put them up on a wall one after the other. The ones that can be done in parallel, can be put in a row above or below the core activities. Once you've completed this, you have a plan! You just need to write it up. If you do this on a chart with some dates on it, you can see when the training can actually take place. You may be surprised how long it is going to take. This should not be a problem. Having a realistic timeline means that you are less likely to have to move the dates back or cancel events, which would damage your credibility and that of your training. The other advantage of this methodical approach is that, if you are realistic about how long each activity will take, based particularly on your actual available time, rather than how much time you would like to have, you are likely to put yourself under less pressure, than if you do not have a plan.

Suggestion 6: Find your champions

Even if you are the chief executive of your organisation, as I have mentioned, I would suggest you need other people to help you introduce mindfulness.

If you are not the boss, it will be equally important to identify who will support you. This may be with financial authority, voicing support in team meetings or just taking part themselves. Your champions may not be the people who become your network of people who are comfortable leading practices or training. This may be because your champions are very senior and may not have the time to train others in mindfulness. Also, your champions may be willing to go so far as to support your trying this stuff, but may not have the confidence to directly put their credibility on the line, by leading an actual practice. That is absolutely fine. You will need supporters in different roles and with different skill sets to embed mindfulness into your organisation. But, of course, if your champions want to become your trainers and leaders, that could also be absolutely fine.

You may also look for champions from different parts of the organisation, people with different degrees of seniority, different lengths of tenure in the organisation, and so on. You are trying to build a network of credible people who can talk about why they support your mindfulness project.

Suggestion 7: Risks and issues

There are many great authors on risk and I'm not going to rehearse how to do detailed risk analysis here, but put very simply it is prudent to think about what might go wrong and to see what you might be able to do to make it less likely that those things will happen. For example, if you are concerned that the training you have arranged might fail because the trainers are not very good, can you reduce this risk by identifying a highly recommended and creditable mindfulness training supplier? Can you ask to attend one of their training sessions, to see if the trainer is smart, on time, credible. The training may still go wrong, but you will have done what you reasonably can to try and reduce the risk that it will be ineffective.

It may be worth sitting down for an hour or two, with your champions and maybe also some sceptics, to go through the possible risks and the potential actions you could take to reduce those risks.

Issues are easier, in a way, in that they are risks that have happened or are happening. So, if the trainer does not turn up on time, have you got a plan in place to deal with this? Perhaps you have the telephone number of the training supplier to hand and can call them invoking the part of the contract that requires them to supply an alternative trainer within two hours, and then ask the trainees to return later in the day.

The risk management exercise should help you identify what might go wrong, what you can do to stop those things from happening and what you might do if they did occur.

Suggestion 8: Be kind to yourself, this stuff is hard

You are about to try and change the culture of a team or organisation, so be kind to yourself and try not to take things personally. I have already referred to the oxygen mask principle and the idea that we need to look after ourselves in order to be able to effectively help those around us and that includes to be effective at work. This is pertinent in your case for mindfulness, because it starts to address the claim that people do not have time for it, but it absolutely applies to you too.

There will be challenges and setbacks and you need to be able to create some space and be a bit kind to yourself, if you are going to see this through.

Suggestion 9: Don't take it personally

Accept you will not win everyone over, but be open to being surprised by the people who do come on board! It may not always be the people you expect who become your strongest advocates. I once went on a tour of locations talking about bringing teams together, who did very similar jobs, to improve the way they worked. There were no job cuts involved – it was genuinely about improving the service delivery. I brought the various sets of two teams together around the country and on more than one occasion there would be one or two people sitting (often in the front row) scowling at me with their arms folded. They didn't like me, what I was proposing or what I represented. Frequently, by the start of the afternoon session those same people were the strongest advocates of the proposals. For years I struggled to understand what was going on. My conclusion was that these were just very passionate people. At the start, they passionately opposed the proposition and by the end, the passionately supported the change.

Suggestion 10: Evaluate

We have already addressed the need to set out the expected costs and benefits of this work, but it is worth revisiting this. One thing that can happen with projects is that they fail to be properly evaluated. Once the project has ended, people move on and there is sometimes no one left from the team to test whether the activity delivered the benefits that were promised. This is difficult for a number of reasons. First, the people whose money you have spent, don't know if it was a good investment. This is not reasonable and it also leaves them with no idea as to whether they should support other similar investment. If your introduction of mindfulness has some of the similar positive outcomes as the (approximately) 4,000 studies that have been completed, why wouldn't you want to celebrate it and indeed take some credit?

The feedback form for the first course I taught posed the question: How important has the course been to you? The scale was 1 to 10. Ten was extremely important and 1 was not at all important. The average was 8.9 (and 9.5 if you took out an outlier). I could not believe that the few hours I had spent teaching had had such an impact on this disparate group of people. It inspired me to continue teaching and helps me to make the case that the courses have an impact on the lives of team members who receive them.

People, particularly people who are spending money, like data, so the more you can build your own evidence base, the easier it will be to keep rolling the activity forward and maybe build on what you have already done.

9 Even more about implementation: practical tips

The previous chapter set out some high-level suggestions on how to plan the implementation of organisational mindfulness as a project. But there are other practical suggestions that might be useful, if you are aiming to create a mindful workplace culture.

Start a conversation

Make sure your whole team are invited to the party. Team events are ideal for this sort of thing, but if you don't have those or if people are geographically separated, you may want to consider how you could communicate the mindfulness news. This could be through newsletters, the blogs of senior leaders or webinars. Whatever tools your organisation are familiar with, I'd suggest you use them. And be prepared to listen, you may be surprised by both the level of enthusiasm and interest and, in some instances, the resistance.

Practical application

There is no point in doing this, unless there is some practical shared practice at some point in the organisation. This does not have to be long practices, or even that frequent, but they do need to be regular and meaningful. The example of the senior management team approach I have shared may be a good example for you. A three-minute practice routinely (weekly) at the start of each senior team meeting could be really impactful. The wider this application goes, the better. The project I have described had at least three management tiers. If each of those groups of team meetings started with a three-minute practice, that would have maximised the impact and therefore the benefit.

Train trainers

Even in small teams, I would suggest that having more than one mindfulness trainer would be beneficial. It removes the risk created by a single point of failure and spreads the responsibility for maintaining the mindful culture. It also reduces the time impact on one individual. If you are in the position to pay for full-time mindfulness leads and teams, as some organisations are doing, you will need to ask people with full-time roles to take on the mindfulness teacher positions.

Have a wide range of champions

Champions are key to this approach; I will say a bit more about this is in the next chapter, but you need senior people to say publicly – this is OK and we support it. Such a role is only in part delivered by supporting funding. It is much more powerful when a senior leader very obviously states their support for the mindfulness approach and more powerful still when they take part and talk about the benefits.

Drop-in sessions

Give people the opportunity and time to go and practise some mindfulness during the course of their week. This may be at the start of the day, or at lunchtime, but having mindfulness going on and available, for people to experience and check out, will make the experience of mindfulness available to the widest possible range of team members.

Consider one-to-one mindfulness coaching

This might be an option you choose to use discerningly, but it may help to have one-to-one coaching for some individuals and you may find it helps win over potential champions. If this seems excessive, a helpful comparison might be executive coaching. Most organisations have invested heavily in their senior people, so it is not unusual for them to receive support from coaches on managing particular pressures or points in their careers. Executive mindfulness coaching is absolutely no different. You are simply providing that individual the opportunity to explore and learn on a one-to-one basis, the tools that can help them to manage stress and improve their ability to deliver to their maximum potential, for example to improve their ability to work collaboratively.

You may not want to restrict this or even apply this to the top team. You may feel this approach is better applied to people who are new to the organisation or people who are actually struggling with stress. As ever, mitigating the risk of their absence from work, may well be worth the investment.

External support

Although this may not always be necessary, or immediately affordable, I do think that my credibility as a mindfulness teacher is enhanced by working with teams of which I am not part. If you exclusively try and bring mindfulness in on your own, people will see you for what you have already been, rather than as an expert on mindfulness. Having an external expert coming into a team and advising on mindfulness techniques and designing mindfulness into ways of working can be much more credible that having an existing advocate pose as the expert. Vishvapani's attendance at the first team event, was enormously helpful in this regard. There are also the time constraints of your existing work, which will make the considerable ask of introducing mindfulness to an organisation hard to sustain. We must also remember (however keen we are) the oxygen mask principle. It won't help your case for mindfulness if you are perpetually exhausted.

With all this in mind, you may want to consider getting an outside voice, even if that is just to start your team on their mindfulness journey.

Communications

Once you've started your conversation, you need to continue it, through the implementation of your mindfulness project and beyond, once you have successfully embedded mindfulness. This could be by setting up fora, working groups, newsletters or using time at follow-up whole-team or local team events. Whatever route you use, I'd suggest you try and make this a conversation rather than a monologue. Find out what more you can do collectively to embed mindfulness. Is there anything that you can do around continuous learning, for example?

We will explore the importance of communication further, particularly around sustaining your implementation. But by involving people and updating them, you can avoid myths and misinformation emerging. You can be transparent about what you are and are not doing and you can bring in more messages from outside to provide reassurance that you aren't doing something completely unprecedented. You may wish to have an article by a person from another organisation that is further down the track of implementing mindfulness than yours. They could provide views on what were the pitfalls, what was the impact? This type of insight can really help people feel they are part of wider change, rather than the change just happening in their workplace.

Mindfulness in the everyday

One wonderful revelation to me when I went on my first mindfulness course, was that mindfulness did not need to be restricted to sitting on a cushion or a formal practice. Making a cup of tea can be a wonderfully mindful experience, as can walking around a park or the streets close to your office (whilst being aware of traffic). So, you may want to introduce mindfulness in everyday life, as well as elements of more formal practice. You may want to encourage team members to take mindful moments in the normal course of their day. Go for that mindful walk around a local park or make that cup of mindful tea.

The point again is this does not have to be hours added onto or taken out of the working day. This is stuff that can be done all the time, as we are doing tasks that we have to complete in any event. The overheads are low for this implementation. It is more about having the courage and imagination to bring mindfulness to the whole workplace. This can include very ordinary moments that we all may just miss, unless we bring our attention to them.

Imagine you've done this

What might your workplace look like after you have implemented a mindful culture? Well, depending on the size of your organisation, you could find that you have a group of maybe ten people who have done sufficient training to lead sessions and they take it in turns to run a morning and a lunchtime drop-in mindfulness session. Not only your senior team meetings, but all team meetings start with a three-minute practice. New starters are introduced to mindfulness as part of the team ethos and invited to try some online or one-to-one led practices, if they are interested. The one-to-one sessions could be led by one of your ten trained practice leaders. You may have a mindfulness forum, where ideas to develop personal and team practice are explored, including references to new articles, or mindfulness activity that other places are trying. At whole-team events, you routinely start your event with a ten-minute practice. People in the team feel comfortable taking their time over making a cup of tea or taking a break from their desk to mindfully walk around the nearby park and anyone who wants to explore mindfulness further is given access to fuller training.

Have a think about how that might feel different to your current working environment. Do you think it's worth a try?

10 Pitfalls and barriers: no one said this was going to be as easy as sitting on a cushion

As stated earlier, this is potentially about culture change, which is really hard to do. I have listed below some of the obstacles that I think you may face as you make a start. This is absolutely not intended to put you off, just to be honest. I've tried to include ideas on how to overcome the challenge too and above all, try to remember that the benefits as they start to flow could be dramatic for the organisation and the individuals within it.

Perceptions

Despite its recent increased popularity and numerous books and support for the subject from high-profile and even royal practitioners, let's be honest: mindfulness and meditation are still seen as being a bit odd (at least in the UK). I was discussing this with friends recently and whilst we reached no conclusion, we suspected that it may be because the first time that western culture became aware of mindfulness or meditation was during the 1960s and the counterculture summer of love malarkey. The association with the Beatles in their hippy phase, Woodstock, drugs and free love may have been well founded in the 60s, but even though we are hurtling towards the 2060s, these associations do not seem to be going anywhere. To be fair, they are reinforced routinely in films and TV shows and there is not much going on to set the record straight.

I think there may be another reason that the idea of meditation or mindfulness still feels countercultural. There are two strong ideas that have dominated in western societies for centuries: self-determinism and rationalism. The first, the bedrock of capitalism, that we should strive for our own personal success and that individually we can and should achieve financial security. The second, that there must be a scientific rationale behind an approach or an activity. Mindfulness, with its associations with a countercultural ideal, may seem to contradict those principles.

Indeed, there is sometimes a debate in mindfulness circles (yes, there are such circles and very serene they are too ...) about whether compassion is an essential part of mindfulness. (Personally, I think it is.) And if it is then what on earth has it got to do with bond trading or running a manufacturing business in a tough global market. How can mindfulness with its "take a breath" attitude, possibly resonate in a "lunch is for wimps" world? I was surprised recently when I was having lunch on a weekday with a friend of mine who is a lawyer and referred to the "lunch is for wimps" culture as being anachronistic and his response was "well, lunch is for wimps really".

There is also the harsh reality that mindfulness is seen as coming from other cultures. Buddhism, of course, is the religion that, in my experience, people in the west associate with meditation. Although Christianity and Islam have a strong meditative tradition, I do not think most westerners would associate those faiths with meditation. For lots of reasons then, meditation and mindfulness is not seen as being "home-grown". It may be seen as being other, from another place.

Finally, and this may come back to its association with hippies and mystics, there is the question of proof. Where is the evidence? In societies that can sometimes pride themselves on their secularism, any association with religion and any idea that mindfulness is an unproven act of faith, is bound to raise the hackles of many.

Being honest about where this iteration of mindfulness in the west has come from, its associations with alternative world views and where society is in relation to self-determinism and rationalism, why am I bothering to write a book aimed at encouraging people to bring mindfulness into traditional workplaces run along post-industrial lines?

Well, having been an incredibly cynical leader, who was and remains pretty self-deterministic; having been a person who loved reason and evidence and still absolutely does; having been a person who dabbled in a countercultural lifestyle during my college years (I was an 80s Goth – it worked for Robert Smith, but really didn't for me) and having rejected it and thoroughly embraced the benefits of a really conventional lifestyle; and being a person who deeply respects other people's faith, but who is not part of an organised religion, I see no contradiction between a rational, self-deterministic, secular (or religious) view of the world, and mindfulness.

Perhaps more importantly, I have seen how it works for me and for teams. It worked to reduce my experience of stress. It worked to improve my ability to perform at work. It worked to enable me to be more present at home with my very conventional family. It worked to even make me more fulfilled at work and in my life as a whole. I have seen it work to make a team become more successful! And as for the rationalism bit, which means a great deal to me, as I may have mentioned before, there are over 4,000 research studies that demonstrate that mindfulness can have significant benefits.

If the reality, then, is that mindfulness may make you more effective rather than less and that it really doesn't require the purchase of a kaftan, and if you choose to introduce mindfulness to your workplace and you come up against any of these preconceptions, you will be dealing with good old-fashioned prejudice, rather than fact. This is important to hold onto. As with any prejudice, it just needs eternal vigilance and hard work to break it down and for you to represent the best of what you are trying to introduce. By playing a very straight bat and simply being true to what you are trying to achieve, you are likely over time to win people over. People who take part will notice the difference in their experience. This is why I have suggested that starting small may be an option – get some allies, some advocates who can provide their own stories about how this stuff has worked for them.

The other thing that you may find really helpful is facts! Use the research to support your case. In the UK, if you point out that Oxford University has one of the major international mindfulness research and training centres, it has an impact! Again, in the UK, if you point out that Cranfield and Ashridge Business Schools have conducted research into mindfulness and found that it works, then you are referring to places that are credible and that adds credibility to your case.

If you are faced with prejudice, my suggestion would be to use evidence, credible association and persistence to overcome it. Do not be frustrated that some people will not come onside. As I have said, it is essential as more and more people find the value of mindfulness, to create space for people who are not interested and choose not to practice it. The task for today may be to just get a foothold and to start to change the culture of your organisation. Initially perhaps with just a few processes, maybe a product or two and a few people, and then building acceptance, based on the evidence and learning that come with your changes.

Time of others

The next, and probably actually the most strongly voiced resistance to mindfulness, is that we don't have time for it. People lead incredibly busy lives and it is hardly surprising that we are not greeted with open arms if we are seen as adding to people's to-do list. When I have been at my absolute busiest, I have made time for a short practice in the mornings. But I have had to get up very early to do that and I accept that that is not going to be possible for everyone. But the reason I did it, was because for me this was part of my survival. Part of staying well. Going back to the oxygen mask principle, if I don't look after my mental health, then I am going to rapidly return to being stressed and ineffective, which doesn't work for my employers or my family.

There is an analogy with the physical gym here. If I stop going, guess what: I put on weight, I feel less well. I get more tired more quickly. If I don't find time for my mindfulness practice, I am less effective. So, finding time, actually creates time. It helps me to work more effectively and that means that I can get out of the office sooner.

This may still be a hard sell, so my suggestion is: don't try to convince people to sit on a cushion for 20 minutes every day. See if you can encourage people to have a three-minute practice at their desk at the start of the day. Emphasise the practical, pragmatic nature of mindfulness: the fact that you don't need a physical room with lots of expensive kit or a membership. You actually carry the one bit of kit you need around with you all the time – your attention!

You may well find that people are really keen to explore mindfulness and are happy to give up time, but for those that are resistant because they feel they do not have enough time, again, I'd suggest you start small and let them see the practical benefits of a few breaths and a mindfully made cup of tea and see where that leads them.

Your own time

Unless you are able to appoint, or become, a full-time mindfulness lead for your organisation, you are always going to face the challenge of competing priorities. We need to be careful here, not to take on or create a role that could easily become full time and just add that to our existing workload. This will simply lead to exhaustion and probably disillusionment. Whilst our ambition is to integrate mindfulness into the workplace, in the processes, products and people's ways of working, initially there will be an overhead of preparing evidence and probably business cases to justify introducing it. You may have to lead a couple of practices yourself, or meet external providers and arrange for them to attend, getting dates in the diaries and organising communications. All this activity takes time and it needs to be factored into your existing diary.

My experience suggests that this becomes a little easier the more senior you are in your organisation. Whilst your workload may be immense, you may also have more control over it and may be able to de-prioritise other activities, or do this in combination with something else, perhaps as you set up staff engagement activities or something that you feel will be addressed or improved by the introduction of mindfulness. This could become your corporate contribution. I may, of course, be wrong, not knowing your personal situation, but the key thing is to make space for the additional work and not to try to be heroic about it.

Less senior folk may be more likely to have a boss scrutinising their activity and delivery on a more detailed basis. If this is the case, I would encourage you to explain what you are planning to do early. Do some planning and explain what you would like to do and how much of your time you think it will take and how you think you can make that work with your current priorities. You may want to choose a time which is a bit quieter in your organisation's business cycle. If you are in an accountancy firm, for example, I'd suggest you don't propose this work stream as you approach year end. You may also know that a project is coming to an end and before you are given a new project, or in the gap between projects, you may suggest that you would like to do some work around engagement and resilience using mindfulness and would your boss be interested in supporting this work before the next project starts?

The main thing, I think, is to be transparent. Don't leave your boss to discover that you have been doing something extra – make sure you have cover to do this new and exciting thing, that is aimed at the corporate good.

Above all, plan. Make sure you know what you want to do, how you intend to do it and what resources (above all your own) will be involved. Then, work out how you can fit that into your workload without creating an unbearable stain or impacting on delivery of the day job. Discuss with peers or bosses or, if you are the boss, your senior management team, so that people are aware what you are doing and you have the chance to get people onside from the start and have a degree of cover for the enterprise.

Money

As I have mentioned, it may be very sensible to get external help for this work, particularly if you are working for a large organisation. The benefits are clear. External trainers should have much more experience than you. As long as you go for accredited trainers, you will have people who have been taught how to train and who have a mature practice themselves. They will also have the time to do this work – that's what you're paying for, as well as their expertise and experience. They will also not be you! They will have the advantage of coming from the outside, so it feels less homespun or made up by a person you know in another context.

The one problem in that paragraph is the phrase, "this is what you are paying for."

As mindfulness has become increasingly desirable for businesses, the provision of mindfulness coaching and training has become professionalised. Quite reasonably, people expect to be paid a commercial rate for the provision of this training, which can transform lives and teams. This means that you will need a budget, if you are going to use the experts.

There has been a tradition of looking to well-being budgets for HR departments to provide some mindfulness coaching. Whilst I am sure it is not universally the case, often well-being budgets can be seen as a soft target for cuts.

You may need to be creative about where you try to find your funding. Leadership training is often seen as something that should be protected, even in difficult times. So, too, are staff engagement activities. The rationale I think is that we still need to develop leaders and have our people onside to get through difficult times. Without wanting to overstep the mark and move into ethically difficult territory, you may also want to see if there is benefit in associating mindfulness coaching with resilience and improved decision making, particularly perhaps in sectors like law, finance or medicine.

One of the many wonderful things about mindfulness is that there is evidence that supports its positive impact in many areas of essential workplace activity. Not just well-being. So rather than try to pin your hopes on getting funds from a constrained well-being budget, is there another programme that has some money? I have normally seen the areas of the business that are generating the most income, or that are seen as creating the next generation of leaders, as being the best funded. So, work with the culture of your organisation. What does the organisation aspire to achieve? What are they prepared to invest in? Get your evidence base together to show that mindfulness has helped other people achieve those outcomes and then propose that some of that budget could be productively spent on mindfulness training.

Timing is important here, too. You may have a culture where there is always money to spend at the end of the financial year, or the start of the financial year, and this may be the best time to propose a budget line. Maybe discuss this with your boss or the finance team to work out what would be most helpful to them. Finance teams hate surprises, so working with them may be a way forward.

Mockery

In tougher environments, you may experience some mockery or teasing. In my experience, this has been good-natured and has just required me to develop a banter to demonstrate that I am not taking myself too seriously. However, I am sure that it could become more than that. You are trying to introduce something new and some people will feel threatened by it. I would suggest again that getting some allies who get this and with whom you can share any challenging experiences might be really helpful. Always remember that you are the one who is benefiting from mindfulness, those who scoff are not. Apply mindfulness techniques to the issue. It may not have been the first time that you have faced a challenge at work, and your mindfulness practice may be the best way to manage any feelings of doubt or fear. If this works, then your adversary is unwittingly providing you with more evidence that what you are doing is right and will help others facing other challenging behaviours in the organisation.

It is worth remembering that, if there is an aggressive or bullying culture, it is likely that this will become harder to sustain as more and more people start to practise mindfulness. Those who are out of step, will simply look increasingly ridiculous.

You may also want to gain support from groups outside your organisation. In many countries there are a number of networks that exist to support and share best practice, the most recent research and ideas. I know that this type of external support has been enormously powerful for individuals who have struggled in their own workplace. It has given them strength to keep going, to a point where they have become enormously successful, leading large, international networks of practitioners. There are some links in Appendix B to groups that may be of help.

But also, be prepared to step away. This is an amazing offer you are presenting to your organisation and the people in it. Ultimately, if they are not ready for it then you may be spending all your time, energy and courage on a hopeless cause! It may just be better to remember the cliché that "discretion is the better part of valour" and take your amazing offer to another place that is ready to take the next step. Whilst I would absolutely advocate the need for courage and determination, this should not become a soul-destroying, endurance exercise.

What will the clients think?

To some extent this is part of perception, but I wanted to call this out, as it is something I have been aware of when pitching for programme management work. I have sometimes been nervous about advertising the fact that mindfulness training is one of the things that I can offer, when the client is a very delivery-focussed project manager. What has really surprised me is the way that people have responded to that offer. People are often much more interested in the mindfulness service line, than the project and programme management ones, with which they are very familiar.

You will know your clients, so you will need to make a judgement about whether the fact that you are bringing in mindfulness is likely to be an asset in those conversations or not. But my suggestion is that you may be surprised how many clients respect the fact that you are trying at least to deliver the widely understood well-being benefits for your teams, even if they are less familiar with the structural approach.

You may need to draw boundaries around where you share your mindfulness practice. If you have meetings with external people who are not part of your programme, you will need to decide how to manage those situations. You may want to include them, briefing the people involved that starting a meeting with a three-minute practice is something that you do and invite them to join you. Or you may not. You may just decide that the implementation of the mindfulness programme is just for internal consumption, so meetings with external people should be excluded from the programme.

Ultimately, you are aiming for the pragmatic introduction of organisational mindfulness and for that introduction to be a success; so, if people are feeling uncomfortable, then it's probably not the right approach.

Getting carried away

Depending on your experience and relationship with mindfulness, you may find yourself getting overly enthusiastic on the subject. I am not suggesting that you shouldn't be keen! That's essential. But it is easy, once you have experienced the benefits of any life change, to become evangelical about it. For months, I encouraged everyone I knew to try the 5:2 diet, unwittingly suggesting all my friends needed to lose weight …. If you have just come through a really stressful time and discovered mindfulness, which helped more than you could have imagined, you can quite understandably find yourself with an evangelical zeal. Whilst this makes sense to you, it can be really off-putting to your co-workers. Better perhaps to consider how you would have reacted to someone with that level of enthusiasm, before you had seen the benefits yourself. Perhaps consider what approaches sparked your interest. For me, it was just the calm demeanour of a friend who suggested mindfulness, rather than a campaigner committed to saving me from my stress.

You may also discover that as the mindfulness work starts to take off, you find more and more opportunities to practice it and lead groups. Again, if you are enthusiastic about the subject, you will want to get involved, but you hopefully still have a day job. It is only fair that if you have agreed with your boss, or if you are the boss, that you will be diverting a fixed amount of your time, resource and energy into the mindfulness activity, that you stick to that. For the early phases of the implementation, you should keep to what has been agreed, else you risk a dip in your performance of regular tasks and this will be seen as a consequence of your involvement in mindfulness. In turn, this impacts on your reputation and the reputation of the mindfulness project.

If you reign in that desire to do more and stick to what you have agreed, you may well find that the success of the first phase of the mindfulness project leads to greater latitude in the amount of time you are permitted (or want to spend) and the budget for future phases grows.

Final note of caution on this point. Even if you are afforded greater latitude and more money for later phases, take a moment to consider if this is the path you want to take. If you want to become a corporate mindfulness trainer, or any other kind of mindfulness trainer, then that is great, and a challenging but fascinating career could await. But if you actually want to be a lawyer, accountant or project manager who uses mindfulness in their workplace, make sure that committing more time to the introduction of mindfulness to that workplace isn't negatively impacting on your core career path.

External scrutiny

Because of the legacy impression of mindfulness, its association with counterculture, hippies, and so on, the thought that it could actually enhance performance and productivity is anathema to some. For people who are highly critical of investment in innovative solutions, the fact that time and money may be spent on mindfulness training, may be seen as a soft target. This can create nervousness among senior managers and a reticence to fund this work, in case it becomes a public target.

I think there are a few ways to tackle this. My preferred way would be head on. The idea that this is hippies on cushions is out of date. There are mindfulness programmes in highly successful businesses like Google and Jaguar Land Rover. The US military uses it for goodness sake, and however else they might be perceived, the idea that they are soft, is not one of them. I would love to see organisations being completely open and saying in newsletters that because of the evidence of its impact on cognitive ability and sick absence, a mindfulness programme is being initiated. If the press or shareholders challenge the spending, the organisation's press office should not be defensive, but should have the extensive evidence to hand and should ask the journalists whether their organisation has a similar programme and if not, why not ... surely their job is stressful?

That said, I am a realist, and this may not yet be possible. Whilst, again, I do not in any way promote being disingenuous, if you have already determined that your organisation's culture would be more likely to support and indeed fund mindfulness training in support of improved decision making or resilience programmes, then it strikes me as entirely sensible to develop decision making or resilience programmes that use mindfulness techniques, rather than exclusively provide mindfulness training. Should the organisation then be criticised for running mindfulness programmes within other training, the courses can be accurately defended by referring to the evidence supporting the use of techniques that improve decision making or resilience.

Essentially, if individuals wish to criticise an organisation, they will do so and will use whatever means they have. My view is that we need to be resilient in our defence of the evidence. This stuff works, we know that. Our competitors or other successful organisations are using it. Should we miss out on the benefits because of the risk of ill-advised criticism?

If this is not your decision to make, you need to make sure that you have the support of whoever can make that decision. It will not help you or your project to be "found out" by the media and criticised and for the senior team to be unaware that this has been taking place. However, if you are open about the benefits, the risks and the mitigations to those risks, and if those who can decide to take that risk sign up to the programme, then if there is criticism, you can be as prepared as possible and ride it out, in the knowledge that the evidence is with you and so is your senior team.

For me, the main considerations are: don't naïvely think that mindfulness will meet with universal external approval; be open about the risks to your senior team (whatever your role in the organisation); be prepared for the challenge in case it comes; and then, do it anyway.

The unexpected

There are normally events that are unforeseen, which present a nightmare for project managers. You do all this planning, you do your risk analysis, you put in place all your risk mitigation and then something completely unexpected emerges and knocks it all off course.

If you are planning your mindfulness programme and then suddenly there is a merger with another business and all the senior team who supported your approach are replaced, you will need to regroup. Similarly, on a smaller scale, if you are about to roll out the training and there is a storm or an interruption to travel services, so no one turns up, you will need to regroup.

The good news is that because of your personal mindfulness practice, you may be uniquely placed to navigate the programme around the unexpected. Be true to mindfulness. Use the techniques that you have applied to the rest of your life to this challenge. Pragmatically and sensibly face the issue. Do you need to go through the approval process again? If so, how do you stand people down from the current training plan in a way that minimises the impact? Do you need to reframe the evidence you have gathered for the new senior team, so that it resonates for them? Or do you need to reschedule the training and get messages out to your delegates as quickly as possible, so they know you know they won't make it and that that is OK?

Whatever needs to be done to deal with the unexpected, I have found mindfulness to be a wonderful tool that enables me to cope and build the confidence of my teams, peers and bosses, in a way that I just did not do before.

An adverse reaction

Very occasionally, an individual could have an adverse reaction to mindfulness. This has not happened in my experience or to the vast majority of people that I have met, who train in a corporate setting. However, it is possible, so it is worth just holding in mind. It could be that a person suffers from a mental illness and symptoms of that illness are prompted by the mindfulness practice.

If you are intending to lead something like an in-depth eight-week programme for your teams, then you will want to simply screen the participants to check whether they are suffering from any mental health issues for which they are currently receiving treatment. You will, of course, need to treat this information with the utmost confidence and need to reassure them of this. You will also need to comply with any local legislation regarding data compliance. But it is better to ask, than to find you are not actually helping the individual.

If, for example, an individual is suffering from depression, then it is sensible for them to check with their medical practitioner as to whether they would be advised to steer clear of the mindfulness training.

You will also want to establish what provision is available for health referral within the organisation. For example, in the UK there are an increasing number of organisations who have mental health first-aiders. If there is in-house provision, you need to know how to contact the person whose responsibility it is to take care of anyone who falls ill in the office. If there isn't any in-house support, you will want to know the procedure in case someone falls ill. In this regard, it is no different from any other training, in that sometimes people do fall ill during training courses as they can do in any other area of work life.

In the rare event that a person does have an adverse reaction to the training, my suggestion would be to simply stop the training and attend to the person who is not well. You may need to end and reschedule the session. The main thing is to make sure that you support the person who has had the adverse reaction and that they get the help they need.

Hard cases

There may be some people who just don't buy this
stuff. As we have explored, there may be many
reasons. The thing to bear in mind is that this is not
an exercise in rescuing people, though some people
may feel enormously helped or rescued. This is an
exercise in introducing tools, to those who are willing
to pick them up, that can help people and the
business. As we've said, you can't compel people to
be mindful. That's just weird. You can only offer
these tools, remembering that part of the mindful
culture that you are developing is to acknowledge
that you have a rich, diverse group of team
members. Some of whom won't want to get
mindfulness.

I once heard a really enthusiastic team leader go
around their team asking what the highlight of their
week was. One person, with no sarcasm in their
voice, just said: "another five days nearer to
retirement". Clearly that person only had one aim in
their career, to get through to their last day in work
and start claiming their pension. It was slightly
heartbreaking and I did spend more time than was
healthy working out how they had become quite so
disenchanted, that they couldn't even be bothered
to lie about something. But ultimately, that wasn't
for me to fix – it was his stuff and I hope he has since
enjoyed a long and rich retirement. Basically, I don't
think he would have been at the front of the queue

for mindfulness training and that's fine. Others will be.

My suggestion would be to invest your energy where it will be most impactful. It is very likely that there will be plenty of people who are interested and who will want your advice, help and input. Leave those who are not interested in peace. There is a risk that you might start to badger them, putting them off even more, or get into difficulty with people complaining about your approach.

If you are clear that this is an optional toolkit, for people who are interested, then it is up to the individuals in the business to pick up the tools.

Geography

If your organisation has multiple sites or people who work flexibly, it may be hard to get everyone together, or to organise training courses where people are physically present. This is not necessarily a problem at all. I have taught one-to-one, full eight-week courses online with great feedback on the flexibility and adaptability this route offers. The training needs some adaption, but many professional trainers will be able to help you with this and will offer an online training solution. Reaching groups is also completely possible through webinars. Whilst I'm trying to avoid lots of data evidence in this text, you may be interested in the research by Cranfield

University who conducted a randomised controlled trial (RCT) in a global firm, measuring the effects of a six-week mindfulness course delivered by Mindfulness at Work: 265 employees were randomly assigned to face-to-face or online mindfulness training, or to a waiting list control group; both face-to-face and online participants benefited from the mindfulness training in the same way.

So, you may find that using your IT systems enables people to access the training that you provide more easily and you may want to bear in mind that the Cranfield study is a helpful reassurance to anyone who may suggest that people have to be trained in person.

For me, the key here is flexibility, accessibility and recognising the different ways in which people actually work. It is important to be as inclusive as possible, whether that is about making sure that similar levels of training, advice and guidance are provided to different sites or about arranging the timing of the training to account for school runs and elder care. We are trying to present pragmatic, practical tools to people that they can take into their everyday lives, so respecting the pressures of those everyday lives from the outset is a good place to start.

And there may be more …

I have no doubt that this is not a complete list of barriers and obstacles. Some will feel unique to your organisation, even though they may not be. Some may be obvious and you may wonder why I have missed them. Unfortunately, this could probably be quite a long section. But, as I have tried to think of some of the challenges that you are likely to face and which feel familiar to me, there are some common solutions or approaches that seem to keep cropping up.

These are my ten tips specifically for overcoming these challenges:

1. Try not to be on your own: there are many, many people out there trying to do the same thing – you may want to connect with them to get that sense of support.
2. Learn from others: both within and outside your organisation – you do not need to have all the answers.
3. When considering the people element, do not get lost in trying to "convert" people: you are offering tools that people may or may not pick up; some people will resist the whole idea and that's fine – that's their stuff, not yours.
4. Remember that you are doing something that is still relatively new and most pioneers have found challenges; that's not a reason not to do it.

5. This could be a culture change and if it is, it is hard, so be kind to yourself.
6. Ask a professional – whilst, of course, being aware that trainers and training firms will be wanting to sell you services, most will be happy to meet to discuss the challenges you face and offer some advice.
7. Innovate: you will want to make sure that what you are teaching people is mindfulness, but with embedding these approaches into the processes and products of an organisation, you can be really inventive; however, make sure the solutions fit the organisation with which you are working.
8. Listen to the challenges, even when they are uncomfortable: there may be important signposts to how you can improve the offer.
9. Celebrate and share success: you will have triumphs as well as challenges, so share the positive moments both inside and outside your organisation. Others will be keen to draw strength and confidence from successes that you have enjoyed, as well as wanting to learn what has worked.
10. Apply mindfulness principles yourself: it is so easy to lose track of our own practice when we are under pressure or trying to achieve something. Make sure you take the time to be mindful yourself.

11   How to sustain organisational mindfulness

I have already referred to the challenge of sustaining this change and I'm keen to spend a bit more time on this theme here. If you and your co-workers are going to go through the process of introducing mindfulness and changing the culture of your organisation, it would be such a waste if the benefits were to wither away once the implementation is completed. It is important that you consider before you even start to implement, as you implement and after implementation has been completed, how to secure the changes that you have made. Your aim here is for the organisation and the people in it to reap the benefits and this should not be restricted to the duration of your stay in the place, or the length of the implementation project.

Advocates moving on: develop a pipeline

One of the biggest challenges to implementing new ideas in corporate environments, is that when the advocates of the new approach leave, the enthusiasm that sustains the new way of working leaves with them. Let's be honest, it will take effort to get this going. If you want to have a sustained impact on the culture of the organisation, how are you going to maintain that effort?

Well, happily, if you have adopted the processes, products and people approach, you have done a lot of the legwork already! The difference between organisational mindfulness and training some mindful people in an organisation, is that you are embedding mindful activities into the very fabric of the place. It is no longer some people who are personally mindful. The way that people do their jobs encourages and, ideally, requires a mindful approach: the shared attention; the reflection; bringing people fully into the room before the start of the meeting.

So, making sure that the processes and the products are fully adopted and implemented, is important. At this point, apathy becomes your friend. Once your processes and products are the standard ways of working and the standard templates on the IT system, then it will take the conscious will and effort of someone to change them. Having experienced how hard it has been to make even incremental changes, you know how much less likely it will be that someone will be willing to change them again.

We have also talked about advocates or champions. These are important for many reasons, including our own moral support. But one of the more frustrating things about people is that they leave. This may well happen to your champions, so it is important to continue to build and refresh your champions group. Don't let it become an exclusive clique, as this will put people off as well as limiting the possibilities of people coming in with their own new energy, experience and enthusiasm.

Something that is also important and may help with generating your new champions and advocates, is induction. As new people join the business, make sure that somewhere in their induction, there is an introduction to mindfulness and how it works in the organisation. If induction in your organisation is very light touch and consists mainly of a tour round the office, awkwardly being introduced to people who don't know what to say, then make sure you or one of the champions are one of those people and make sure you or the champion does know what to say about mindfulness in the organisation ... at least. It might be the most reassuring introduction they get. If induction is more structured and consists of presentations or training, then make sure that you or one of the champions gets a slot at the induction session. You may want to include in that introduction the opportunity to become a mindfulness champion.

As with all mindfulness training, I would suggest that you don't assume zero knowledge. People have often come across or used mindfulness, as we have discussed before, so in either structured or unstructured induction, it's a good idea to establish the level of understanding and experience of mindfulness of the individual or group and then adjust your presentation accordingly. But, still explain why your organisation has bothered. What you mean by organisational mindfulness. The areas where a person will see a difference from other organisations. I might even refer to processes, products and people, so you can share some examples. Even if it is quite early in the roll-out of mindfulness for your organisation, I would suggest that time spent setting out what is happening with the mindfulness programme and encouraging them to become a part of the change, is time very well spent. Again, part of this process is normalisation, so the more you make this approach standard, for new people as they join the organisation, the less grafting on of a new idea you will have to do in the future. New people won't see this as new to the organisation and indeed, many apprentices, school leavers or graduates will not see your approach as novel. The use of mindfulness techniques in the way your organisation works will just be the way it is.

In addition to your core supporters on the shop floor, and unless you are the chief executive or a member of the board, you will benefit from having champions in the boardroom or in the top team. If you do have senior champions, you need to be aware that they will often move on rapidly too. You would therefore be well advised to have more than one board-level mindfulness champion and some sort of succession plan, even this is just in your own mind, about who will step in when your senior champion goes. This is critical. If the mindfulness programme is just seen as the pet project of one or two individuals and they go, it could be seen by a new senior team as faddish and an opportunity to sweep it away. For it to truly become part of the DNA of an organisation, you need as many of the top team to buy into it as possible.

My suggestion would be to talk to your senior champion, or if you haven't got one yet, then identify a person that you think could become that person. Explain what you are trying to do, how you want it to be sustained after both you and the senior champion have gone and ask them for some insights on the rest of the top team. Who else might help or be interested? How could you get them to a training course? Who would they feel comfortable advocating to for the programme? Whoever they think are your best bets should be in your mind for your succession plan and you should consider carefully their advice on how to approach them.

If you are the CEO or the top team mindfulness advocate, then you may have a fair idea of when you are moving on. You will hopefully know who else in the top team to approach and who is likely to support you and the programme. I'd suggest you would benefit from having frank conversations with your peers before you embark on bringing mindfulness into your organisation; through these conversations, you are likely to identify your successor for the mindfulness programme. At the right time, discuss with them the possibility of them taking over that role.

You moving on: succession planning

To some extent, if you have embedded mindfulness in the processes and products of the organisation and you have got people openly talking about and advocating mindfulness, then whether you are the senior champion or the programme lead or both, your leaving should not be the end of the story. As I mentioned, apathy to some extent becomes your friend, in that people will be unlikely to revisit and change processes and products that have recently been refreshed. But you may have been more important than you realise in giving others in the team the courage to talk about and practise mindfulness.

It may be that people feel it is safe to be mindful in the organisation, because the trailblazer is there – partly because you took the flack and were willing to do the work to establish the ways of working, but also because, however democratic or inclusive you have tried to be, this is to some extent your vision! When you go, it is likely that people will feel the absence of their mindfulness leader.

How best to defend against this? Again, I think this comes down to succession planning. First, you need that network of advocates whilst you are initiating and implementing the programme, for all the reasons we have already explored, including your sanity. But they become even more important for the organisation as you move on. You need to know that enough people are sufficiently knowledgeable about the processes and products and why they exist as they do, and the way that they promote and support shared experience, to be able to maintain the evolution and improvement of the structures. If what you have achieved stagnates, it will risk becoming irrelevant. For example, as new processes come on stream you will want your champions to make sure that the organisation's mindfulness approach is applied to those processes.

I'd suggest you also need people who have a sufficiently well-established personal practice to be anchors to the whole endeavour. You need people who can continue to be the advocates and probably the only people who can really do this are those who have benefitted from the practical application of mindfulness. You also need these people to be the ones who can answer the questions of those who are new to the subject – they may be in-house trainers too or they may be the people who hold the relationship with your external trainers, coaches or advisors.

For all these reasons, a strong network of mindfulness advocates will be key to sustaining the programme after your departure.

Programme plan

Another idea might be to agree with your network of advocates a programme of mindfulness-related activities, or change that extends beyond your tenure in the organisation. For example, you may have in your sights other processes that could do with a mindfulness review. Agree with the process owner when the process will be considered and put that into a plan. You may have a mindfulness seminar in mind – book it for after you have left. Has the organisation signed up to more training? Are there any team events planned and will one of the advocates be willing to speak at those events? Are the induction sessions booked and do they have mindfulness materials or speakers present? Any activity at all that you have in mind, or that can be agreed (including funding) prior to your departure, should be captured in a plan spanning out as far as possible. Twelve to 18 months would be a great ambition. Then get this plan signed off by the top team. This will mean that the top of the shop has bought into the idea that mindfulness will still be part of the organisation long after you have gone. They also have something that they can refer back to and can support your advocates in delivering, or indeed challenge them, if they are not delivering.

If you have gone down the formal programme route, this becomes easier because, unless you have closed the programme and moved onto a "business as usual" footing, you will hopefully have a replacement for the programme manager who will simply move into that role. But if – as I suspect, most of the time – programme management approaches are supporting a more organic implementation, then having a plan that senior people expect to be delivered plus people who are keen to deliver it, is a good way to keep the show on the road.

Evidence

Evidence and evaluation have cropped up a few times – the strongest reason for mindfulness to be sustained in an organisation, must surely be that it works. It is also a good way to get increased financial backing. Home-grown evidence is an enormously powerful tool. So again, plan how you are going to gather your evidence and evaluate your programme before you start and then make sure you have factored in the time to gather and analyse the data. If you are able to demonstrate tangible benefits, whether a drop in workplace absence (and the associated cost saving) or an increase in staff engagement scores (on which many businesses place a premium) then the people accountable for cost saving and staff engagement will be keen to sustain and possibly extend the programme.

If you have the evidence of the benefits, then not only are you demonstrating that the changes you said would emerge in your initial pitch are materialising, but you are also demonstrating at a very practical level that this is not about hippies and cushions. This is not made up or mystical. This stuff has a practical impact, having been pragmatically applied, and you have taken the time to measure the impact. Your proposition that mindfulness can transform people's work life has home-grown evidence to prove that this has happened. Powerful, and hard to dispute.

Inviting some of the people who have been affected by the mindfulness approach, particularly process and product owners, to come and speak to the top team to explain the practical impact, could also be incredibly persuasive and help support the presentation of the core data. You may find some of your harshest critics, become your strongest advocates.

Of course, if you are able to bring mindfulness to the top table itself, both through training the individuals and perhaps starting their meetings with a three-minute practice, then you may find that your strongest advocates and the reason the mindfulness programme is sustained, is the top team itself.

Communication

I've mentioned the importance of normalising mindfulness. For me, it doesn't matter what terms you are using, but bringing the principles of mindfulness into everyday conversation is a powerful way of saying that this stuff is normal and is a part of the way that we are going to work. So, too, are examples of successes or innovations. It is quite possible that when you start your programme, you have a lot to tell people about forthcoming training events or revisions to processes or products, and it could all feel quite new and exciting. But, as mindfulness becomes mainstreamed and you have properly embedded the transformation, there may be less to say. It's important though to keep the conversation going. It would be easy for it to slip off the radar and apathy could allow old habits to return. My suggestion would be to mainstream the communications around mindfulness, but to make sure that it still has a presence. If you have a newsletter for the organisation, for example, have a mindfulness column and use that column not only to update people about the current mindfulness activity that is going on in the organisation, but link it to other activity of other businesses. Once again, yours will not be the first organisation to introduce mindfulness. There are many large organisations that have already done a lot of this work. Using an established network, you can find stories from outside your organisation, that provide insights, ideas and inspiration. It can be really helpful to know that others are applying these principles. As well as learning from their mistakes and successes, it just continues to normalise the approach.

Lessons learned/annual review

If you have implemented your organisational mindfulness approach as a programme, you will want to do a closure report. In the land of programme management, this is when you are closing down the temporary organisation (the programme) that you set up to deliver the change and handing it over to the parent organisation. The report summarises how the programme has gone, what has been achieved, how the money has been spent, and so on. It should also include the outcomes of a "lessons learned" exercise. This report can be the perfect opportunity to make recommendations to your senior team, on what should happen next. How can this be sustained as part of the "business as usual" of the organisation?

This report can be a good place to recommend what needs to happen to make sure that the benefits expected from this investment are being realised.

My suggestion would be to have a team made responsible for producing an annual (or even quarterly) report on the health of organisational mindfulness within the organisation. This report must, of course, be proportionate to the size of the organisation. But what is achieved here is the creation of a deadline, a cycle and an accountability. The nominated team will have to gather data to be able to complete the report. The sensible way to do this is to gather the data throughout the year, rather than try and do it in the last week. This then creates a responsibility for the nominated team to effectively assure the activity of whoever is actually now responsible for mindfulness in the organisation. If this is still you, then that's fine, you can help them with the data, but the difference is that this is a task that part of the existing business will have to pick up, after the programme has closed.

If you haven't run the introduction along formal project management lines, you can still nick the idea. So, once you feel comfortable that you have trained all, or a fair proportion of, the people you wanted to train, and you have got a few processes and products in place, you may want to step back and produce a report for the top team, to demonstrate the progress and again to suggest the next steps to further embed these ideas.

All you are doing is applying the principles behind organisational mindfulness. You are creating a moment of shared attention where those ultimately responsible for the budget and the organisation's culture, or your senior team, if you are the boss, can bring their awareness to what has been achieved and what you want to happen next and who you want to do it.

External networks

As more and more organisations start to introduce mindfulness, the networks that support mindfulness practitioners are growing. I have already suggested that this might be a good place for you to look for advice and support. It is also a good place for your organisation and the people in it to find the support it needs as it moves forward. These networks can provide stories for your ongoing communications, speakers for team events and advice on how to continue to develop these approaches.

Keep innovating

To date, there is nobody to tell you that you have done it! Whilst there are organising bodies who can accredit trainers, there isn't an equivalent to certify that yours is a mindful organisation. No one can tell you that you have finished, but to be honest it feels contradictory to everything I know about mindfulness to suggest that there is an end point. There isn't, as far as I am aware, a finishing line for my personal practice, so why should there be one for organisational mindfulness? I have advocated a programmatic approach to implementing organisational mindfulness, but this is because there are certain elements of programme management methodologies that work really well for delivering change. Once the implementation has been largely done and you are looking to sustain the approach, I would suggest you try to keep it fresh. What else are other organisations doing that we haven't tried yet? Can we share some of our best practice with them? Are there areas of the organisation that were in the "too hard for the time being" camp that we can now look at?

If you keep evolving the thinking, the design and the processes, you will make sure things don't get dull and are more likely to keep people's interest.

Be true to the ethics

Authenticity and consideration for others in the organisation will always be key. If you are to sustain the approach, you need to continue to demonstrate the values that we have mentioned. You need to be considerate of others and their reticence to take part. Failure to do so is likely to create resentment and call into question why you or your successors are doing this. You also need to make sure that your successors have the same authenticity that you have. You will want people who practise mindfulness themselves, understand its value and how the organisational mindfulness that has been built in your organisation works, so that they can talk with confidence and conviction about the organisational mindfulness approach.

It is also important that the approach is not exploited to try and coerce people to do more for longer. As already discussed, this is not the point of the exercise. If people see that organisational mindfulness is actually being used to get more for less from the people in the organisation, it will soon lose the support that you have built and it will be rejected.

Keep a record

You would be wise to record the changes to processes and products that you make and the training that you provide, as you go along. Whether or not you are running this as a programme, the knowledge of what went before, the changes that have happened, why and what they have achieved, will help people in the future understand what has been done. This is crucial. Without effective corporate knowledge and knowledge systems, people can find themselves grappling with what has gone before and why a certain practice is the way it is. Omitting to explain the reason for a change can lead to confusion and risk the change being unpicked – by anyone who can get over their apathy. It is vital for all of this to keep developing and evolving, but why allow all the work you are doing to be lost? The conversations with the process owners, the results of any pilots … if you record this information in an easily accessible and understandable way, then you may be saving someone else from making the same mistakes that you have made. You may also enable your successors to build more effectively on what you have done, and make it harder for people to undo your work, because your rationale and the work you have done with your colleagues will be evident.

12   Reflections on implementation of a mindful programme

I have been enormously fortunate to have had the opportunity to try to implement organisational mindfulness. Below, I have set out a few remaining thoughts from my experience of going through this process.

Time

I was the programme director for this programme, which meant that my job was very highly pressured and time-consuming. In turn, this meant that I did not have as much time as I would have liked to extend the mindful culture. Most of my time was spent with the senior management team and this meant that most of the mindfulness activity that I led was with that team. I would have liked to have spent more time with a broader range of team members, to be able to offer them more experience of mindfulness, perhaps having teams other than the senior team start with mindfulness practices. It would have been great to have been able to lead mindfulness drop-in sessions as well.

More teachers

As the sole mindfulness teacher in the team, I was the only person who felt qualified to lead mindfulness practices. This clearly restricted the number of groups that could be led. Looking back, if we had had the capacity, establishing a group of people who could lead the mindfulness sessions across the programme would have been a great asset. It would have meant that a wider set of people would have been able to experience mindfulness directly in their immediate teams, but also it would have made certain that the mindful culture was not at risk, should one individual leave. Training more mindfulness practice leaders, would have helped to embed structural mindfulness and ensured that there were many people rather than one person to maintain the energy.

Sustainability

Building on the previous point, one of the key reasons for trying to establish a mindful team, rather than just a number of mindful team members, is to make the application of mindfulness sustainable. I have set out in some detail how I think the sustainability challenge could be overcome, but it is worth repeating that its survival and capacity to thrive after the initial protagonists have left the organisation will be one of the key challenges. I am sure I have not always achieved this as successfully as I would have liked.

Induction

We did a lot of work on induction to the team, but we hadn't perfected that aspect of our processes before I left. The way people arrive in an organisation is so crucial to how quickly they can start to deliver and thrive. An introduction to mindfulness, as part of our induction process, would have ensured that new joiners had a clear understanding from the start that mindfulness was part of the culture and that the offer was available to them, should they wish to participate.

Churn

It was personally quite hard to maintain the focus and application on mindfulness as some of the key advocates left the programme and new team members joined. This made maintaining the momentum tough. To some extent, the answer was simply to be fairly tenacious and relentless. To go again, as new people joined. But if we had had more people delivering mindfulness training and leading mindfulness sessions and if we had mindfulness as part of the induction process, I think the application of mindfulness would have been less dependent on individuals and therefore more sustainable.

13   Authenticity

One quality that I feel is essential to applying mindfulness in the workplace, is authenticity. Desperately trying and failing to avoid the joke about "once you can fake authenticity, you're sorted". But, most of us are not RADA-trained actors, so if you are not actually practising mindfulness yourself, then it must be harder to bring other people on a mindfulness journey. Your examples will be out of date, your demeanour is less likely to be convincing and ultimately, you will start to doubt your own message.

Since taking this stuff up and integrating it into my life, numerous colleagues have commented on how I have been calm in stressful situations. When I talk about mindfulness, people do not generally question the honesty of what I am saying or doubt that I am authentic. They can see the practical benefits embodied in the way I deal with the same stuff with which they are grappling.

This is not to say that I am always calm, let alone serene – of course I'm not. But people see me as being authentic, even if they can't see how they might apply it, because this stuff works and they can see that I am applying it.

I suspect that this is essential for the first advocate of mindfulness in your organisation – you. But, as we will explore later, you will need other champions. And it will be important for people to see that others are also putting mindfulness into practice. A massive step forward would be the senior team. If the top table are starting their meetings with a three-minute practice, then it becomes very hard for the naysayers to say that it is not credible, or not to be taken seriously. If the people who ultimately hold the purse strings for everyone's next pay rise are visibly backing and, more importantly, practising mindfulness themselves, then you are sending a strong message that this is for real.

In a super-cynical observation, it is likely that some more junior leaders will want to emulate the bosses, so they are seen to be doing the "right thing". But this kind of activity also does much more than entice mimicry. Perhaps, most importantly, it will start to have an effect on the senior team. My experience was that the team I was part of became more collaborative, supportive and creative as well as just present in our meetings. It may start to affect the behaviours of some of the senior leaders. The Cranfield research talks about leaders listening to people differently and asking the expert! It also starts to build personal stories among your leaders. So, how powerful is it to have a member of the board stand up and tell the rest of the organisation about the impact of mindfulness on their work life? Well, again, from personal experience I would say immensely powerful. Many people will see it as being a tool in the armoury of achieving and sustaining a senior post, so it is something that becomes admired and respected, rather than just a bid odd. There is also something very powerful about senior leaders demonstrating that they experience stress. Of course, not all of your senior leaders will want to, or feel comfortable with, doing this. Indeed, if you are a senior leader, you may not wish to do so. But, if one or two senior leaders feel able to share the fact that what we do as an organisation is hard and stressful and that since mindfulness has been introduced they have used it effectively to help cope with that stress, then many others in the organisation will respect that and your implementation will become a whole lot easier.

I'll always remember the first time I, as a director in a large organisation, stood up in front of 70 people and spoke about my mindfulness journey. How the stress had got too much and how I had reached out to a friend who signposted me to mindfulness. During the break, another leader came up to me and thanked me, saying how powerful it was to have a senior leader talk about mental illness. A chill ran through me and I thought: "I didn't! Did I?" It hadn't been my intention, but I guess I had, even though I hadn't described it in those terms. What was more important was the reaction of the individual. He had heard a senior person talk about their experience with stress and how mindfulness had helped them.

Three key thoughts, then. Make sure that you are actually practising mindfulness. It is harder to sell a product that you don't believe in. Not impossible, but harder. If you are practising it, then it will be more likely that you are benefiting from its proven advantages and others in your organisation will probably see that.

The second thought is to try and gain advocates. People who can join you in supporting organisational mindfulness and tell authentic stories of their own about the benefits that they have experienced.

Third, if you can get your top team to start doing some mindful things, then that is enormously helpful. If they can personally become your advocates for mindfulness, then that's great. But also, for the organisation to see that some mindfulness concepts are being adopted and put into effect at the very top, will be a powerful signal. I would suggest that even if the top team do want to become your advocates, you will also want others who may be more credible and relatable to the teams affected.

14 The importance of people who do not want it

It is important to consider that compulsory mindfulness is not possible as far as I am aware, let alone desirable. Requiring people to bring their attention to the breath, apart from it being somewhat difficult to detect defiance, would be unethical if it could be achieved. But, I want go further than this. I have come across a number of people who did not like or want anything to do with mindfulness. Something just doesn't sit well with them or, in some instances, it has felt like it strays into religious territory, which either feels uncomfortable because the person does not have a faith and has no intention of taking up mindfulness as an alternative, or because they do have a faith and they feel that mindfulness is in conflict with it.

I am very comfortable that the mindfulness I have experienced has been entirely secular. But that is absolutely not the point. People have a right and legally recognised right (in the UK) not to be discriminated against because of their faith or lack of faith. It is therefore essential that people do not feel under any pressure whatsoever to take part in a mindfulness practice. This may feel contrary to your ambition to establish a mindful environment, but being mindful of people's alternate view is entirely consistent.

In a working environment, where people are often under pressure to conform and where you have managed to get senior leaders to support your mindfulness agenda, it is even more important that people do not feel pressured. There are a number of ways that you can try and avoid this from happening. First, make it clear from the outset that mindfulness is optional. State this emphatically in your first communications about this work and repeat it often. Make sure your senior leaders mention this in their communications as well.

If you are successful and mindfulness practices are at the start of the agenda for most team meetings, then you may have individuals who do not take part. That is absolutely fine. In most work-based practices, I start the practice by saying something like, "and if you don't want to take part, that's absolutely fine – if you could just sit quietly, that would be very much appreciated". It is fair enough to look to those individuals who do not want to take part to show the participants in the mindfulness practice the same respect that they have been shown.

To date, I haven't come across anyone who feels so uncomfortable that they have felt they can't sit in the same room for three minutes. But if this does happen, I would suggest that they routinely join the meeting five minutes from the start so that they miss the mindfulness, but not the second and subsequent agenda items.

I think there is something important here about not making people feel uncomfortable if they do not want to be involved. As mindfulness becomes more and more part of "the norm" for all the reasons we have discussed (introduction in schools, productivity, well-being and personal benefits, etc.), it is vital that we do not push people who do not want to participate to the margins. People may choose not to take part purely out of cynicism, or because they feel it contradicts their religious faith or for any number of other reasons. That must be fine. We should not let enthusiasm for a new way of working and being which could be full of compassion become a route for new discrimination and exclusion.

15   Collaborative working: shared decision making

Your organisation may well not go in much for shared or collective decision making. If it is a very top-down or command and control organisational culture, then it may feel that this is less relevant; but in my experience of incredibly intense and pressured command situations, the risk assessments that are made to inform command decisions, require a shared view. This may ultimately be a majority decision, but the data has to be jointly analysed, views need to be aired and then a judgement made on the right advice to be given to the decision maker.

Whether this is similar to the way your organisation works, or whether you have a more democratic environment, being able to see the data in front of you clearly for what it is and for all to see the same data, is vital. But how often do we achieve this? I once witnessed an extraordinary demonstration of how two sensible, intelligent groups of people, taken from a shared environment, can see data in entirely different ways.

A friend and co-leader and I were designing an away-event for our team. I asked a great trainer that I had worked with for years to help us and to do some work around Myers-Briggs type indicators. For anyone not aware, Myers-Briggs assessment are a way to identify certain preferences for the way your team members see the world. People are grouped according to certain categorisations, for example Introverted or Extroverted, Feeling or Thinking. The team of about 30 people were asked to complete questionnaires in advance of the event and were given their reviews. This gave people four letters that very broadly indicated each individual's way of experiencing the world. Mine was ENTP: Extrovert, Intuitive, Thinking, Perceiving. Our trainer asked all the people who had been assessed as Thinkers to move to one corner of the room and all the Feeling types to move to another corner. He gave each group the same picture and asked them to write up what they saw.

The Thinkers wrote things like, "There is a river, there is a boat on the river, there are three people in the boat, there are trees by the side of the river". The group with the Feeling preference had phrases that I remember distinctly, including, "The wind is howling" and "God is in the sky". Some of the Thinking preference group were incensed! Where could the other group see from the picture that God was in the sky! It was infuriating for them.

The key point for me was that these were two groups of sensible people with a shared task who had seen completely different things from the same picture.

If this was possible for a picture of three people in a boat (I was in the Thinking preference group), what chance do we have of seeing the same thing in a complex, nuanced piece of policy advice or high-pressured operational situation? Could it be possible that by using some mindfulness techniques to try and come to a non-judgement or at least "less-judgement" based understanding of the facts that are presented to us, we are likely to be able to bring our expertise more dispassionately to bear on the issue at hand? Could this lead to better-quality decision making?

I think this is what lies behind the reports of increased collaboration among teams who use mindfulness. The judgement and prejudice about a subject that we all routinely experience, normally completely unwittingly, can be diminished if not overcome. If we collectively have a shared experience of some information, rather than separate and potentially conflicting experiences of our own prejudices, then we are starting to look at the same thing. Which, in itself, feels more collaborative than not understanding why the other people in the room can't see "God in the sky" or that there are just "three people in a boat".

16   Work–life balance: another view

I have intentionally focussed on the workplace in this book. There are far better qualified authors who have written amazing books on mindfulness for the individual. But there is a particular area I would like to explore a little, where the personal and professional life of people meet. This is sometimes described as work–life balance. This term used to be very much in vogue in the 90s. In essence, the idea, as I understood it, was that people would be more effective in the workplace, less likely to be stressed, burnt out, if they balanced being in work with healthy pursuits outside the workplace, whatever these might be. It did, of course, depend on the "life part" not consisting of spending the whole weekend in the pub, or indeed finding your home life so intolerable that you would rather be at work. But the idea had, to my mind, a lot going for it. For most of us, being at work 12 or more hours a day will not be sustainable physically or mentally and will have a detrimental impact on our personal lives.

This phrase seems to have been more recently replaced by "presenteeism" – the phenomenon that people feel they have to be in the office and be seen to be in the office in order to progress in the organisation. The use of language, I suspect, is to make it resonate with bosses who see absenteeism as a bad thing.

I completely agree that a balance in our activities is important, but I remember being astonished when a director colleague, who I knew had a rich range of commitments outside the office, including charity work and a young family, said that he didn't see a distinction between his work and his life. Work was part of his life, as were the other activities and the rest that he enjoyed. He felt it was an artificial distinction.

I think both the arguments for work–life balance and the point that the distinction is artificial can be true and I think they neatly highlight something interesting in relation to mindfulness.

We know that just being in the office all the time is likely to be bad for our health. But, for me, drawing a line between the two and saying work and life are separate things, runs the risk that I will start to see work as a negative and life outside as a positive. This is simplistic and might find me counting down the days to my retirement …

Mindfulness might be able to help bring the two thoughts together. By noticing what we are actually experiencing both inside and outside the workplace, we can start to recognise our whole life for what it really is. It will include difficult bits and joyful bits, whether they are in work or not. We can also fully notice when we are experiencing exhaustion and step back from the brink (or preferably way before the brink) so that we can rebalance our experience; and we can make those choices whether the exhaustion is being generated by work, or indeed, from our life outside work.

So, by being more completely aware of what we are actually experiencing, we can start to make better choices about what will actually sustain us, not based on a work/life division but by truly recognising what will actually give us some balance.

17   Shopping lists: the whole of your life

I have tried to be disciplined in writing this and to stick within the bounds of workplace mindfulness. The notable exception might have been the chapter on work–life balance. But, as I was considering that chapter and the chapter on programme management as a mindful practice, it occurred to me that it is not just the workplace that gives rise to mindful practices.

We have numerous, almost in-built parts of our personal lives that you could (if you wanted to play fast and loose with definition) consider to be mindful practices. We could ask why we have shopping lists – clearly, it is to make sure we don't forget anything that we need while we are in the shop. That's great and certainly part of it. But if we take the time to bring our attention fully to what we need for the week ahead, is this not a mindful moment? If we then ask other people in the house or the family to contribute to the process – "Jack, is there anything you need from the shops?" – is that not an attempt at achieving shared awareness? Just as I used the holiday example to demonstrate programme management in action in our home lives, I think we can consider the shopping list done by the family or flatmates as an example of shared attention.

There are loads of examples, once you start to look for them. The parents stopping their child just before they hurry off to school: "Giselle, have you got everything?". The parent is creating a pause. The attention of both parent and child are being brought to one issue – it is being shared. There may be judgement, but there is an opportunity for non-judgmental present-moment awareness.

Going back to the holiday example. What about the shared decision making, if there was one? Here again, the family or friends are brought together, structurally to try and consider the options (the data) and reach a shared decision. This feels to me like an opportunity for very judgmental present-moment awareness – "but I want to go to the beach ...".

I am mentioning this to advance the case just a little further that mindfulness is instinctively part of how we operate. We create structures to achieve personal or shared awareness, but then we might not always implement them as well as we could. We might come to better and more shared decisions if we apply some of what we have discussed here, to these mindful moments. Again, we can do so pragmatically and practically. We may choose to do this just for ourselves, rather than propose the teenagers should join in. But it is worth experimenting with these approaches in all facets of our lives.

One of the attributes that, for some reason, I did not expect to find with mindfulness is that for me, it is cumulative. If I do it regularly, for long periods of time, I become more creative and better able to cope with stress. I discovered this long before I had the courage to take mindfulness practice into the workplace at even a personal level, let alone at an organisational level. But if I stopped doing it, then in just a few days I would be rattier, less calm, less able to cope.

If you do bring mindfulness practice into your personal life, you may find that the consequences for your workplace practice and experience is profound. As well as being less likely to forget the milk from the weekly shop.

18   Not to forget well-being

I have intentionally tried not to focus on the well-being benefits of mindfulness. Again, there are other books and evidence that explore this area fully. But having benefited so much personally, and having seen the impact on other individuals and teams, it feels remiss of me not to mention it at all. I do not want to delve into the reasons why it works, but my personal experience helps me to refocus when I meet barriers to introducing mindfulness to teams, or when I feel a bit under siege. As I said at the start, when I discovered mindfulness I was not in a good way. Having said a bit more about my experience, it may become clearer how mindfulness helped me.

Seven years ago, despite having a great job, a wonderful wife and family and good health, I felt overwhelmed. I did not feel like I was achieving enough, financially, or in the work I was doing. I was full of fear, mostly irrational, but even the fear about things that might have happened was overwhelming. I felt I had been overlooked for promotion and wanted a higher status job, with more responsibility. I was struggling to hold down my own job. I was distracting myself with alcohol and socialising. This made everything a whole lot harder, not easier. I was regularly hungover going to work and was often out socialising when I should have been at home with my family. The spiral, that will be familiar to many people, seemed inexorable.

The difference that seems so obvious now, but that hit me as a revelation when I started practicing mindfulness, is brilliantly summed up in the expression that Breathworks (the amazing organisation with whom I trained to become a trainer) use in their course:

"Thoughts are not necessarily facts"

This expression seems so self-evident, but for me it was very powerful. The thoughts that I was professionally missing out, that I was failing, that something would happen to me, my wife or my children. These thoughts owned me. They ran my head – completely dominated. It was hardly surprising, then, that I had little space in my mind for effective thinking about the things that I was actually concerned about: work or family. It was also hardly surprising that I sought out anaesthetic from what was a very painful place to be.

Before I ever heard the phrase that to me explained what was going on, practising mindfulness helped me see my thoughts differently. I could step back from them and not be carried along by them. This was such a shift. It didn't and doesn't stop those thoughts emerging, but their force is completely different.

I share this rather personal experience, because I know that it is not unique. People I have trained and shared some of this thinking with in work teams, have had the same lightbulb moment as we start exploring these ideas and some people have shared that they have had similar experiences of being overwhelmed by their own thoughts.

This is how mindfulness helped me to get out of a dangerous and self-destructive mindset. But I appreciate, whilst my experience was not extreme, you may be reading this thinking that I just needed to get a grip, and that this does not relate to you as you have not had this experience. If that is the case, that's brilliant for you and my suggestion would be that the techniques offered by mindfulness can help you to stay in that fit position.

If you have ever lost your temper when driving and thought afterwards (even if you have not admitted it to yourself at the time) that you were a bit over the top; or had a conversation in the office that you thought was out of order and dwelt on it all day, into the evening and even had trouble sleeping; or been enraged by something a relative has done and you have not been able to see past the fury, to the point when you feel like you never want to talk to that person again – if you have experienced any of these things, or if there are any other examples you can recall when, once you have calmed down, you think … that was a bit over the top – then these may have been instances where your thoughts have been running you, rather than you being able to step back and take a more dispassionate view. Or, to put it another way, to have been non-judgmentally aware of the present moment.

If this resonates at all, then you may find that mindfulness may have something to offer you personally. Even if it doesn't resonate, but you think that it sounds like someone or some people in your teams, then you may find that mindfulness has something to offer them. There may be people you are aware of, who have had to take time out because of stress; you may be aware of people who you know are under stress, but have not yet got to the point where they have to step away. You may have some people who just seem to be under a bit of pressure and you may have some colleagues who are doing fine, genuinely, but have very stressful jobs. All of these groups might benefit from getting a different perspective on their thoughts. This is, to me, the core of the well-being reward from mindfulness – whether that is helping people recover from stress or providing an additional toolkit for people who are thriving and who want to stay that way. The key that can unlock the change, is to consider our thoughts as things we can watch, rather than things by which we are carried away.

If you think that your organisation could collectively make better decisions and be a less stressful environment; if the people in it and the processes and products used, helped people step back and see situations for what they actually are, rather than what your collective or individual thoughts are all telling you; then organisational mindfulness may be useful to your business in the way it conducts its work and may also help support the well-being of the well people in your organisation, as well as those who are struggling.

19   Conclusion: so what could you achieve?

What might change if you implement this approach? Well, we have covered a lot of the possible benefits of the application of a mindful approach as we have gone along. It is very likely that the individuals who have taken part in the programme in your organisation will feel better: emotionally, intellectually and physically to varying degrees. The stress of working in your working environment will not have evaporated, but they are likely to be better able to cope with it and less likely to be adding to it. As a result of being able to choose where they bring their attention, rather than being at the mercy of their thoughts, they are likely to have a more realistic and manageable perspective on what is going on for them.

This could help some people who were really struggling to stay in work and stay working with you. This could help them and your organisation, by avoiding the costs of retaining the skills that already exist and avoiding the cost of recruiting and retraining. It could help those who are really starting to feel the pressure to avoid the crisis that so many experience in work; again, helping them and the organisation by avoiding the emotional impact of the crisis (for the individual) and the cost of cover for the organisation. It could also have helped those who currently show no signs of fatigue or the impacts of stress, to stay well.

From this description, you might sense that this approach could enhance the loyalty of the people in your team. The organisation has chosen to invest in their well-being. Provided training, knowledge and space to help them in life. That could well show up in your staff engagement scores and the reputation or your organisation as an employer. In turn, this could have a significant impact on how attractive your organisation is to the employment market, particularly as the next generation hits the workforce.

As well as improving the well-being of your people, you will probably have helped improve their decision making. If they continue their practice, the research shows that there are likely to be increases in cognitive ability and creativity as well increased productivity through fewer sick absences.

My experience, though, is that the most evident, powerful and perhaps transformative change that I have seen in a team, is the collaborative working. Shared experience, shared attention may achieve two things: a greater sense of joint endeavour and a feeling of mutual support. These are important, because the whole decision-making team are taking the decisions based on a shared view of the world and because less energy is wasted in blaming and scheming, and actually seeing different things. This no-longer lost energy can be ploughed into effective leadership.

Leadership itself in your organisation is likely to be improved too, as the Cranfield studies have shown, with a greater likelihood of the experts being heard and the leaders being able to listen. There is even a greater chance of your people sticking around through adversity.

You will have made this change sustainable, not dependent on you or your initial advocates to keep the changes going and you will have embedded the principles and the ways of working into the very way that people do their jobs and the materials they use to do it, by enhancing processes and products as well as introducing ideas about mindfulness to the people in the organisation.

Do these incremental changes sound to you like they add up to a more productive workplace?

What you will not have achieved is for everyone to have joined in. I may be being unfair – I don't know your organisation – but I suspect there will often be people who choose not to participate. I would suggest that is fine, so long as they don't get in the way of those who do want to engage. But, ultimately, this is their loss and they may come round in the end.

You will not have banished stress or indeed the cross word from your organisation, but you are likely to have reduced the stress levels in the organisation and, in part, this may have been down to fewer cross words, misunderstandings and moments of madness. You may also have just opened up communication in your organisation in a way that allows people to express their frustration, before it becomes an issue.

You will probably not have gone for the cushions and very low desks approach. I may be wrong, and if you have and that is right for your organisation, then fab! But what you are more likely to have done is demonstrate that organisational mindfulness is practical and has tangible benefits that support, rather than undermine, the core objectives of the organisation.

You will not have felt totally on your own, because both within your organisation and outside, you will have found numerous people who are interested, willing to help if they can and, if nothing else, share their disasters and triumphs.

If you have been practical, pragmatic and taken people with you, you will not have damaged your reputation. This is not soft stuff and you may well get a great deal of support and increased credibility, because you are bringing in these ideas and because people attribute the improvements in the workplace and in their own lives, in no small part, to the fact that you had the courage to implement organisational mindfulness.

Further Reading

Throughout the book I've identified key people who have either directly influenced, inspired and helped me or who have done so through their writing. Below, I have tried to set out a taste of their work, so that you have an easy place to start to explore their inspiration. But I'd encourage you to search further. This select group have so much to offer.

Vajragupta Staunton

This extraordinary author has numerous books that are a delight to explore – these are just a taste:
Free Time! From Clock-Watching to FreeFlowing - A Buddhist Guide (ISBN: 9781911407249)
Wild Awake: Alone, Offline and Aware in Nature (ISBN: 9781911407188)
Buddhism: Tools for Living Your Life (ISBN: 9781899579747)

Paolo Quattrone

Paolo was key to me understanding that the way we design the products and processes could transform the way we make decisions and run our organisations. The link below takes you to a lecture Paolo gave in 2015, around the same time I met him. It reflects just part of what he taught us; but is a great place to start.
https://www.bing.com/videos/search?q=paolo+quattrone&view=detail&mid=B2514814E831B23A6B45B2514814E831B23A6B45&FORM=VIRE&adlt=strict

Lucas den Engelsman

Lucas has simply been a dear friend and teacher during my journey to become a mindfulness teacher. He is ethical, able to challenge and wise. To learn more about what he is doing, he can be reached through his website:
https://momentful.co/

Vishvapani Bloomfield

Vishvapani has been another friend and teacher. His broadcasts (Thought for the Day, the Today Programme Radio 4) always provoke thought and inspire. His literature should also be explored. *Gautama Buddha: The Life and Teachings of The Awakened One* (ISBN: 978 1 84916 923 3)

Jon Cowell

Jon has been another friend and supporter, who has encouraged me as I've moved from working in programme management to organisational mindfulness. To learn more about him and his company explore the links below.
https://www.sbs.ox.ac.uk/about-us/people/jon-cowell
https://www.edgecumbe.co.uk/

Alison Reid

I have not mentioned Alison directly in the book, but I would like to invite you to explore her work. Alison has been another encouraging influence as I have set up my company Lines of Sight; her understanding on how our bodies and minds are truly interdependent is fascinating and her wisdom around what can help a leader lead is genuinely valuable. Alison's White Paper below is a good place to start:
https://www.alisonreid.co.uk/white-paper/

Vidyamala

Vidyamala was one of the founders of Breathworks with whom I did my mindfulness teacher training. I've since had the privilege of meeting and working with Vidyamala and she is as impressive in person as her reputation suggests. Vidyamala and Danny Penman's book *Mindfulness for Health* has simply changed many lives, but all Vidyamala's books should be explored:
Mindfulness for Health: A practical guide to relieving pain, reducing stress and restoring wellbeing (ISBN: 978-0-7499-5924-1)
Living Well with Pain and Illness: The Mindful Way to Free Yourself from Suffering (ISBN: 978-0-7499-2860-5)
Vidyamala and Claire Irvin: *Mindfulness for Women: Declutter your mind, simplify your life, find time to 'be'* (ISBN: 978-0-349-40852-1)

Jon Kabat-Zinn

A book about mindfulness would not be complete without a reference to Jon Kabat-Zinn and I have used his definition of mindfulness very early on in the book. I was fortunate enough to attend an event where Jon spoke a few years ago and it is fair to say that what I heard that evening was a key motivation for me to write this book. Jon has written numerous books, but you may want to start with: *Coming To Our Senses: Healing Ourselves and the World Through Mindfulness* (ISBN: 0 7499 2588 4)

Jamie Bristow and the Mindfulness Initiative

Again, I have not specifically mentioned Jamie in the body of this book but his work with the Mindfulness Initiative might well be called relentless. I have had the pleasure of working with Jamie recently and his commitment to supporting the development of mindfulness is unwavering. As Director of the Mindfulness Initiative, Jamie has overseen the production of a number of key publications, but the two that have had the biggest influence on my work are: 'Mindful Nation UK' report and 'Building the Case for Mindfulness in the Workplace'. Several of the quotes in the book and particularly those of the Cranfield study, are taken from this publication. To learn more, I'd encourage you to visit:
https://www.themindfulnessinitiative.org/

Nicola Lowit

As I mentioned, without the reassurance and collaboration Nicola provided, I would probably not have started that first drop in session. I am enormously grateful. To find out more about Nicola's work her web-site is to be found at: https://www.nicolalowit.co.uk/

Made in the USA
Monee, IL
24 May 2021

69393321R00114